YOU'RE NEVER TOO OLD TO LAUGH

"Has your grandfather stopped chasing women?"
"No, but we got him to slow down. We took the tires off his wheelchair."

Molly had just turned 90. Her little house was filled with knickknacks and whatnots people had given her.
A friend asked, "And what do you want for your ninetieth birthday?"
"Give me a kiss," she answered, "so I won't have to dust it!"

Watson, a 66-year-old Tampa stockbroker, was pouring his heart out to a friend.
"I'm nuts about this girl," he said. "Do you think I'd have a better chance of marrying her if I tell her I'm 50?"
"I think you'd have a better chance if you tell her you're 80."

Grandpa Palmer was caught unprepared by the Minnesota cold spell last winter and complained to his grandson that he hadn't been able to sleep.
"Did your teeth chatter, Grandpa?"
"Dunno," he replied. "We didn't sleep together."

GROSS JOKES

by Julius Alvin

AWESOMELY GROSS JOKES	(0-8217-3613-2, $3.50)
AGONIZINGLY GROSS JOKES	(0-8217-3648-5, $3.50)
INTENSELY GROSS JOKES	(0-8217-4168-3, $3.50)
INFINITELY GROSS JOKES	(0-8217-4785-1, $3.99)
TERRIBLY GROSS JOKES	(0-8217-4873-4, $3.50)
SAVAGELY GROSS JOKES	(0-8217-5149-2, $4.50)

Available wherever paperbacks are sold, or order direct from the Publisher. Send cover price plus 50¢ per copy for mailing and handling to Penguin USA, P.O. Box 999, c/o Dept. 17109, Bergenfield, NJ 07621. Residents of New York and Tennessee must include sales tax. DO NOT SEND CASH.

YOU'RE NEVER TOO OLD TO LAUGH

Larry Wilde

Pinnacle Books
Kensington Publishing Corp.
http://www.pinnaclebooks.com

PINNACLE BOOKS are published by

Kensington Publishing Corp.
850 Third Avenue
New York, NY 10022

Copyright © 1997 by Larry Wilde

All rights reserved. No part of this book may be reproduced in any form or by any means without the prior written consent of the Publisher, excepting brief quotes used in reviews.

If you purchased this book without a cover, you should be aware that this book is stolen property. It was reported as "unsold and destroyed" to the Publisher and neither the Author nor the Publisher has received any payment for this "stripped book."

Pinnacle and the P logo Reg. U.S. Pat. & TM Off.

First Printing: September, 1997
10 9 8 7 6 5 4 3 2 1

Printed in the United States of America

For Morty Bass,
art aficionado, film fan,
theater fanatic, and
Florida's funniest
retiree

We do not stop laughing
because we grow old—
we grow old because
we stop laughing.

Contents

INTRODUCTION	9
Chapter One: Gallant Gents	13
Chapter Two: Golden Girls	33
Chapter Three: Gleeful Grumblers	55
Chapter Four: Groovy Granddads	75
Chapter Five: Genial Gripers	97
Chapter Six: Giggling Grandcritters	115
Chapter Seven: Gobbling Gourmets	135
Chapter Eight: The Gameaholics	153

INTRODUCTION

> *The young man who has not wept is a savage, and the old man who will not laugh is a fool.*
> —George Santayana

Never before in the history of the universe have there been so many people over the age of 55. By the year 2000, the U.S. Census Bureau predicts there will be 56,000,000 people who fit this description.

These folks, affectionately referred to as "senior citizens," for the first time in history rule the world. They have not only lived longer, possess most of the wealth, and made the greatest contribution to society, but, coincidentally, have the best sense of humor.

Many older people eschew the title "senior citizen." They want to be known as the "chronologically advantaged." Old-timers know the best way to beat the clock is with a healthy dose of wit.

Of course, humor is ageless, but mature adults

respond and react spontaneously to amusing situations with unbridled laughter and genuine appreciation.

Maybe it's maturity, security, or seeing life from a broader perspective. The years have taught older people a lighthearted approach to living. They seem to be better able to laugh at life's mishaps. Age allows us to take ourselves less seriously, to see the brighter side, the funny side of life:

> A reporter for the local newspaper was doing a story on longevity and approached one of the elderly men observing a game of horseshoes in the park.
> "Tell me, sir," asked the newspaperman, "what type of person lives the longest?"
> "A rich relative," was the quick reply.

This book was designed especially for folks over 55. It covers every humorous phase in the lives of the chronologically advantaged, everything you could possibly poke fun at. From loss of memory and Maalox to medication and Medicare to cantankerous grandchildren and dentures to cheating on the golf course.

It's about the human condition, about people who have had the great good fortune to live a long life—through good times and bad—and are able to laugh about it.

Here are the world's best *tasteful* jokes for seniors!

Remember—they're not *wrinkles,* they're *laugh lines!*

LARRY WILDE
Carmel, California

Chapter One

GALLANT GENTS

> At 20 we don't care what the world thinks of us. At 30 we worry about what it thinks of us. At 60 we discover that it wasn't ever thinking of us.
> —Sam Levenson

There was a memorial service being held in a small chapel. Friends of the deceased had all gathered to pay their respects. Several people in the audience got up and eulogized the octogenarian who had passed away. When they finished, the minister said, "Is there anyone else who would like to say a few words?"

There was silence in the room. Then an elderly man down in front stood up and said, "If nobody else is going to speak, I'm a retired broker, working part-time with Merrill-Lynch, and I'd like to tell you about our Tax-Free Investments."

The retirement center band had finished a vigorous and not overly harmonious selection, and as the perspiring musicians sank to their seats after acknowledging the applause, the trombonist asked, "What's the next number?"

The leader replied, "The Stars and Stripes Forever."

"Oh, no," gasped the trombonist, "I just played that."

————

The insurance agent was surprised to find a couple in a retirement village with no insurance. In his effort to sell a policy to the husband, he said, "How in the world would your wife carry on if you should die!"

"Well," answered the husband, "I really don't care how she carries on after I die, just as long as she behaves herself as long as I'm alive."

————

By the time retirees learn
to watch their step, they're
not able to step out anymore.

Florence and Henry finished their breakfast at the retirement home and were relaxing in the library. "You know," said Florence, "today, in most marriage ceremonies, they don't use the word 'obey' anymore."

"Too bad, isn't it?" retorted Henry. "It used to lend a little humor to the occasion."

When President Clinton visited California, he stopped at a San Jose retirement residence to say hello to some of the residents. He was up on the second floor and stopped a woman with snow-white hair. "Hello," said Mr. Clinton. "Do you know who I am?"

"No," she replied with a smile, "but if you go downstairs to the desk, they'll tell you who you are."

A politician was trying to drum up votes at a Seniors' Community Center.

"If I'm elected," he promised, "I'll get rid of socialism, communism, and anarchism—"

"Yeah," interrupted an old man from the back of the room, "and let's throw out rheumatism, too!"

"How come you stopped drinking, smoking, gambling, and cursing?"

"Because that widow asked me to."

"So how come you didn't marry her?"

"Well, since I'm such a clean-cut, decent, desirable man now, I figured I could do a lot better than her."

Did you hear about the 95-year-old gentleman who married the 93-year-old woman?

They spent the first three days of their honeymoon just trying to get out of the car.

The elderly driver made a right turn from the left lane and smashed into another car. The guy screamed, "Why the hell didn't you signal?"

"Why should I?" said the old guy. "I've been turning here for forty years!"

You know how you tell when you're getting old? When your broad mind changes place with your narrow waist.

—Red Skelton

ELDERLY GENT

Just when you're successful enough
to sleep late, you're so old
you always wake up early.

"Reverend, that was a damn good sermon you just gave," said old Smithers to his white-haired minister.

"Thank you, but I wish you'd express your enthusiasm in a more restrained fashion."

"I can't help it, Reverend. It was such a damn good sermon, I put $100 in the collection plate."

"The hell you say!"

OVERHEARD IN A RETIREMENT VILLAGE

First widow: They say he married her because her first husband left her a million dollars.
Second widow: Oh, I don't think he's that kind of a fellow. I think he would have married her regardless of who left her the million dollars.

————

Steve Allen, the brilliant comedian, author, composer, pianist, and TV show host, tells this to his concert audiences:

We're going to find out tonight who the oldest lady in the audience is. And we have a marvelous present for her. When we find the oldest lady, we're going to give her—the oldest man.

The first time we tried this was about ten years ago. We had a very nice lady in our audience. She was 87 years old, as I recall. We introduced her that evening to a man from Chicago who was 96, and shortly thereafter, believe it or not, they were married. It was a lovely story. And that wasn't the end of it, either. I read in the paper recently where that woman has just given birth to a beautiful 47-year-old baby boy!

"Say, Ken, since your grandson finished high school, is he gonna get a job this summer?"

"I don't know. He flunked out as a lifeguard. He forgot to remove his bubble gum during a mouth-to-mouth resuscitation test."

Filmore and Mobley were taking their morning stroll downtown. As they passed a funeral parlor, a procession was leaving, and tears began forming in Mobley's eyes.

"What are you crying for?" asked Filmore, "Was the rich old man who died a relative of yours?"

"No, he ain't," said Mobley. "That's why I'm crying."

Cronin puffed heavily on his cigar while loitering in the shopping mall drugstore.

The pharmacist had to speak forcefully to him, "Please, sir, there's no smoking."

"But I just bought the cigar here."

"Look," said the druggist, "we also sell laxatives here, but you can't enjoy them on the premises."

In Abilene a pharmacist filled a prescription for an old friend.

"Let me know if this stuff does any good, Travis. I've got rheumatism myself."

Mrs. Edelman's son had to attend a pharmacists' conference one evening, so she agreed to work in his Bronx drugstore. Old man Brodsky wandered into the store and said, "How much you charge for a box of Alka-Seltzer?"

"$9.50," said Mrs. Edelman.

"What?" exclaimed Brodsky. "Every other drugstore in the Bronx, I could get it for $6.00."

"All the other stores are closed now. You want it or don't you?"

"How much is a bottle of Maalox?"

"$8.95," said the druggist's mother.

"Are you nuts?" shouted Brodsky. "Anyplace you go in this city, you could get it for $5.50."

"Listen, we're the only store open. Take it or leave it."

The old gentleman bought the Maalox, and as Mrs. Edelman leaned over the counter Brodsky could clearly see the woman's cleavage.

"What's that?" he asked.

"What do you mean, what's that?" said the woman. "That's my bosoms. What did you think it was?"

"Well," said the senior, "everything else here is so high, I thought it was your behind!"

Kimball brought home a swing set for his children and started to assemble it.

After hours of frustration trying to follow the directions, he gave up and called old Swenson, the handyman.

Swenson threw away the instructions and soon had the swing set completely assembled.

"It's beyond me," said the father, "how you put it together perfectly without even reading the instructions."

"Tell you the truth," replied the old-timer, "I can't read—and when you can't read, you've got to think."

Steve Green, the personable prescriber at Optical Images of Carmel, loves this lulu:

Matson complained of seeing dark spots in front of his eyes.

"Glasses should help," said the eye doctor. He wrote out a prescription.

Matson reported back a week later.

"Do the glasses help?" asked the doctor.

"Oh, yeah," said the old gentleman. "I can see the spots much clearer now."

Dalton, the druggist, finished filling old man Pendelton's prescription. He handed the customer a little bottle with twelve pills in it and said, "That'll be $16.50."

Suddenly the phone rang, and as the druggist turned to answer it, Pendelton put 50 cents on the counter and walked out.

Dalton turned around, spotted the 50 cents and shouted after his customer, "Hey, that's $16.50, not 50 cents."

The druggist picked up the half-dollar, put it in the cash register, and said, "Oh, well, 40 cents profit is better than nothing."

— — — —

Horace had been a widower for nearly two years and his friend, Fitz, finally persuaded him to start going out again. "How'd things go on your date last night?" asked Fitz.

"We went Dutch treat on everything," said Horace. "When I got her home, she said, 'Since we've gone Dutch on everything else, you can just kiss yourself good night!' "

Many retired gentlemen still
chase girls but only if it's downhill.

Karinsky was killed in an accident, and Berkowitz, the president of the condominium's Home Owners' Association, was sent to break the news to his unsuspecting wife.

"Be careful how you tell her," advised a friend. "She's a very delicate woman!"

Berkowitz knocked on the door, and she came out. "Pardon me, are you the widow Karinsky?"

"Certainly not."

"You wanna bet?"

The lawyer stood before the family of the recently deceased Moskowitz and read aloud his will:

" 'To my dear wife, I leave my house, fifty acres of land, and one million dollars.

" 'To my son, Allan, I leave my Cadillac and $300,000.

" 'To my daughter, Hannah, I leave my yacht and $300,000.

" 'And to my brother-in-law, who always insisted that health is better than wealth, I leave my sunlamp.' "

Spinelli became incensed when the druggist informed him that his favorite over-the-counter cure-all now required a prescription.

"Mister," explained the pharmacist, "you can't have this except by prescription because it's habit-forming."

"It is not," screamed the old gent. "I ought to know, I've been taking it regularly for twenty-two years."

————

"You're a stubborn old coot."

"Is that so? Listen, I'm so completely open-minded on this issue, that I'll even listen to your fantastically stupid, idiotic opinion."

————

Hanlan telephoned the local undertaker and said, "I'd like to come down later today to make arrangements for my wife's funeral service."

"Your wife?" said the funeral director. "Didn't we bury her three years ago?"

"Yeah, we did. However, I married again."

"Well, congratulations!"

————

There's no fool like an old fool—
unless he's got money.

The groundskeeper at the cemetery heard the cries of an elderly gentleman as he lay across the grave. He was crying, "Why did you die, oh, why did you die?"

"Was that your wife?" the groundskeeper asked.

"No, it wasn't my wife. Oh, why did you die?"

"Was it a friend?"

"No."

"It wasn't a member of your family?"

"No, oh, why did you die?"

"Who's buried in that grave?"

"My wife's first husband."

― ― ― ―

Millie Golder, the matchless Cornish & Carey real estate marvel, relishes this rib-tickler:

Rupert, 83, met Eloise, 81, on an Elderhostel trip to Los Angeles. The night before they were to leave, the old gentleman knelt before his new and exciting love. "I have two questions to ask you," he said.

"Yes," responded Eloise excitedly.

"Will you marry me?"

"Oh, yes," she said, "I was waiting for you to ask me! Now what is your second question?"

"Will you help me up?"

Did you hear about the elderly country-western singer who finally announced his retirement?

His adenoids cleared up.

COUNTRY-WESTERN SENIORS' SONGS

"Since Grandma Shot a Hole in
Grandpa's Head—
It Sure Cleared Up His Sinus."

"Grandma Was a Pippin—Till Her
Uppers Started Slippin' "

Why did God never plan for grandparents to have babies?

Because they might lay a baby down and forget where they put it.

There is good news for seniors regarding memory, hearing, all the faculties. The last to leave us is sexual desire and the ability to make love. Which means that long after we're wearing bifocals or hearing aids, we'll be making love. But we won't know with whom.
—Jack Parr

Bigelow sat reading the sports section when his wife walked in and said to him, "Don't you think I look younger without a bra?"

"You really do, dear," he answered. "It's drawn all the wrinkles out of your face."

Zarrow was 73 and getting married for the sixth time. As he waited for the ceremony to begin, he thought of the songs that had been played at all his previous weddings.

When he married the first time, he was an athletic 20. The band had played, There'll Be a Hot Time in the Old Town Tonight.

Zarrow took his second wife at age 30 to the strains of *I'll Be Loving You, Always.*

At 40, they played, *Now and Then.*

At 50, he had danced to *Don't Get Around Much Anymore.*

His fifth wife had joined him when he was 60. Their song was *The Thrill Is Gone.*

Suddenly his thoughts were interrupted by the church organ, announcing the beginning of the ceremony. Zarrow strode down the aisle as the organist played *Remember When.*

― ― ― ―

Cardiff and McBride, two craggy-faced retirees, were philosophizing on a Coney Island bench. "My son, the 38-year-old genius, phoned this morning," announced Cardiff. "His wife's pregnant again."

"That's nice," said McBride. "But the best time for men to have babies is when they're 80. That's when they have to get up ten times a night anyway!"

Bonnie Gallaher, the clever California conference coordinator, savors this corker:

Slayton, a young minister, was serving as volunteer chaplain at a large nursing home. He had never performed a wedding, so he asked an older pastor what to do in case he forgot something during the ceremony.

"Just start quoting Scripture until something comes to you," said the older clergyman.

Soon Slayton was asked to marry a widow and widower who were both in their nineties. Right in the middle of the ceremony, he forgot what to say next. Remembering the advice of the older pastor, he started quoting the only Scripture he could recall: "Father, forgive them, for they know not what they do!"

On a recent flight to Minnesota, nationally known novelist, Nancy Baker Jacobs, overheard this nifty nugget:

A grandfather on a United flight turned to the occupant in the next seat and said, "Have I told you about my grandchildren?"

"No," said the gentleman, "and I certainly do appreciate it!"

Grimaldi called his neighbor to help him move a couch that had become stuck in the doorway. The two old men pushed and pulled until they were exhausted, but the couch wouldn't budge.

"Forget it," Grimaldi finally said, "We'll never get this in."

The neighbor looked at him quizzically and said, "In?"

Ned and Sandra had just celebrated their fiftieth anniversary. As they were driving across town to their home, she remarked, "You know, we used to sit closer to each other in the car in our courting days over fifty years ago."

"I haven't moved!" exclaimed Ned.

The minister shouted to his congregation: "Stand up if you want to go to heaven!"

Everyone stood up except an elderly man sitting in the front pew.

"Are you telling me you do not want to go to heaven?" thundered the preacher.

"When I die, yes," said the man. "But I thought you were getting up a group to go right now."

RETIRED GENT

Reaching the age where you've got to prove
that you are just as good as you never were.

Phillip and his wife both had hearing problems. "Look," he said, "when I say something to you, for goodness sake, show me that you heard me some way or another."

"Okay," she replied. "I'll tell when I don't hear you."

Age is nothing more than mind over
matter. If you don't mind, it doesn't matter.
—Satchel Paige

Several years after his retirement, Wally wanted to go back down to the office and see how things were going. Just to find out how well he was remembered, he decided to go in and ask for himself.

"Can I speak to Wally Morrison?" he asked a bright young secretary at the front desk.

"Oh," she said, "Wally Morrison doesn't work here anymore."

"Oh," he said, "then let me speak to the man who filled his vacancy."

"Well," the secretary said, "Wally didn't leave a vacancy!"

— — — —

The worst thing about retirement is
having to drink coffee on your own time.

Chapter Two

GOLDEN GIRLS

> *You're never too old
> to become younger*
> —Mae West

Duncan sneaked up behind a blue-haired beauty at a seniors' dance, covered her eyes with his hands, and said, "I'm going to kiss you, if you can't tell me who I am in three guesses."

"Teddy Roosevelt! Andrew Jackson! Abraham Lincoln!" she answered quickly.

Molly had just turned 90. Her little house was filled with knickknacks and whatnots people had given her for her birthday.

A friend asked, "And what do you want for your ninetieth birthday?"

"Give me a kiss," she answered, "so I won't have to dust it!"

"Gramma, can you remember your first kiss?"
"Son, I can't even remember my last one!"

Levinia was telling her daughter about a date with a 90-year-old man. "Would you believe, I had to slap his face three times."

"Do you mean," asked the daughter, "that old man got fresh with you?"

"Oh, no!" said her mother. "I had to keep slapping his face to keep him awake."

Bunny Barb, the merry Manhattan MD's spouse, loves this bit of medical mirth:

Doctor Metcalf confronted Mrs. Tomkins about the bills she hadn't been paying.

"I'm very sorry about this," said the physician. "But I don't see how I can continue to treat you because your bill is much more than it should be."

"Well, I'm certainly glad you have come to your senses, Doctor," she cried. "Now, if you'll just make your bill out for what it should be, I'll write you a check!"

Grandma Esther and her Temple Ladies' Auxiliary were on a tour of Europe. She never stopped complaining about the lack of punctuality of the local guides. As her group stood at Runnymede in England, Esther snapped at the guide, "Come on, begin already!"

"Ladies," he announced, "on this very spot was signed the historic Magna Carta."

"When?" asked Esther.

"1215."

She glanced at her watch. "We missed it by twenty minutes."

Two widows were visiting in the lounge of the Seniors' Center. "Well," one said, "Margaret has just cremated her third husband."

"Yeah, that's the way it goes," replied the other widow. "Some of us can't find a husband, and others have husbands to burn!"

In her will, an unhappy wife requested this epitaph: *After Having Lived with Her Husband for Some 65 Years, She Died in Hopes of a Better Life.*

Joyce Milligan, San Jose's devoted book booster, bowls friends over with this bubbly bauble:

Maude, Penelope, and Doris, three widows, were living together in a house. One afternoon Maude announced, "I think I'll go upstairs and take a bath."

When she arrived in the bathroom, she shouted down to the other women, "Was I coming up to take a bath, or have I just finished taking one?"

Penelope said, "I better go up and help Maude."

She got halfway up the stairs and shouted down, "Was I on my way up the stairs, or was I coming down?"

Doris said, "I'm so glad I've still got all my mental faculties, knock on wood! (KNOCKING) . . . Was that somebody at the front door or the back door?"

― ― ― ―

The grandmother of today has
something that the grandmother of
the past didn't have—blond hair.

"Don't you think Hazel looks very young for her age?"

"Listen, she's had her face lifted so many times she has to walk on tiptoes."

GRANDMOTHER

A baby-sitter who doesn't
hang around the refrigerator.

Loretta, 92, and living in a nursing home, received a visit from Adelaide, whom she had known in the Garden Club.

"Oh," said Loretta, "I'm just worried sick!"

"What are you worried about, dear?" asked Adelaide. "Are they taking good care of you?"

"Yes."

"Are you in any pain?" she asked.

"No."

"Well, what are you worried about?"

"Every close friend I ever had has already died and gone on to heaven. I'm afraid they're all wondering where I went."

Hyacinth and Sybil were sitting on a porch, rocking back and forth in rocking chairs. "Do you ever think about the hereafter?" asked Hyacinth.

"All the time!" said Sybil. "I go into a room and look around and say, 'Now what was it I came in here after?'"

The elderly farm couple sat in their rocking chairs in front of the fireplace one wintry night in Kansas.

"The years are passing us by, Eunice," said the old man.

"Yes," she agreed.

"We're getting older," he said, "and pretty soon only one of us will be left."

"That's right," she said, "and when that happens, I'm moving to California."

"How old do you think that widow Mrs. Whitman is?"

"Her age is her own business—but it looks like she's been in business a long time."

"May I have another cookie?"
"Another cookie, what?"
"Another cookie, please."
"Please, who?"
"Please, Grandmother."
"Please, Grandmother, what?"
"Please, Grandmother dear."
"Certainly not! You've had four already!"

Miss Merilyn rushed up to the policeman. "I've been attacked," she cried. "He ripped off my clothing. He smothered me with burning kisses. Then he made mad passionate love to me!"

"Take it easy, ma'am," said the officer. "Just when did all this take place?"

"Twenty-eight years ago this November," said the elderly woman.

"Twenty-eight years ago!" he exclaimed. "How do you expect me to arrest anyone for something that happened twenty-eight years ago?"

"Oh, I don't want you to arrest anyone," she replied. "I just like to talk about it."

On a windy Chicago street corner, a still-attractive senior citizen held tightly to her hat with both hands while her skirt flew above her waist.

Two men passing by noticed the gray-haired lady struggling with the elements. She smiled at them and huffed, "What you guys are looking at is 68 years old. What I'm hanging on to is brand new."

SATISFIED GRANDMOTHER

If she had it to do all over again,
she would bypass children and
just have grandchildren.

Did you hear about the ingenious Georgia grandmother who devised a foolproof, no-cost security system?

She hung a key by a cord to the front doorknob. Naturally the key didn't fit, but by the time the intruder realized the key wouldn't work, Grandma was out the back door and around the house, holding a shotgun on the culprit.

Clementine and Yancy had lived together for sixty years. Yancy had never forgotten her birthday. However, he noticed the date on the morning newspaper and remembered, "This is her birthday!"

Yancy looked across the table to see if she had remembered. Evidently Clementine had forgotten, too. Sitting there for the next few minutes, their sixty years together passed through his mind. She had been a fine wife all through those years of heartaches, struggles, joys, and victories. Clementine was as sweet and lovely as she was on their wedding day. The only difference was that she had become a little hard of hearing.

Yancy leaned in her direction and yelled, "Wife, I'm proud of you!"

She yelled back at him, "That's nothing! I'm tired of you, too!"

― ― ―

Maurice should have known better when he proposed to Daphne and asked, "Darling, do you think you can live on my pension?"

"Sure," she replied, "but I don't know what you're going to live on."

At a community dance for seniors, Amos, 79, noticed Marge, a very attractive widow in her late fifties, sitting alone. He invited her to dance. In a few moments, they were fox-trotting all over the floor. Amos leaned her over in a dip, and Marge said, "Listen, I'm not interested in getting married."

Amos didn't answer. A few minutes later, he dipped her again, and she said, "Look, I really don't want to get married. Unless you've got $600,000 in cash and a few million in securities."

"Lady, at this moment in the bank, I got exactly $12.82."

"That's close enough," said Marge.

A Phoenix police officer pulled 86-year-old Mrs. Chen Lu over to the curb.

"You weren't using your turn signal lights," he said politely. "First you put your hand out as if you were going to turn left, then you waved your hand up and down, and then you turned right."

Mrs. Chen Lu explained, "I decided not to turn left, and when my hand was going up and down, I was erasing the left turn."

Soon after her husband died, Marlene, 64, decided to learn to drive a car. On her first trip to town, she drove right through a red light. "Don't you know what that light means?" asked an angry policeman. "It means stop!"

"Oh, I'm so sorry, Officer," said Marlene.

"Haven't you ever driven before?" he asked.

"Well, yes and no."

"Yes and no. What kind of answer is that?"

"Well, I have driven before, but this is the first time I've driven from the front seat!"

Mrs. Lefkowitz and Mrs. Fine were strolling the boardwalk in Atlantic City.

"I think older women like us should take a greater interest in politics," said Mrs. Lefkowitz. "Tell me, what do you think of the Common Market?"

"Well, I still prefer the Safeway."

GRANNY

The baby-sitter who
does it for nothing

————

Three Japanese businessmen from Tokyo were strolling along Fifth Avenue in New York City. They window-shopped, snapped pictures of St. Patrick's Cathedral, and were thoroughly enjoying their sight-seeing.

One of them stopped Mrs. Feinstein, a white-haired, sharp-tongued New Yorker. In a strong Japanese accent, he said, "Please, you could tell us how to get to Bloomingdale's?"

The old woman snapped, "You had no trouble with Pearl Harbor—you certainly could find Bloomingdale's!"

————

Mrs. Costanza was proudly wheeling her granddaughter down a Staten Island street. A friend stopped her, peeked into the carriage, and cried, "Oh, my! You got some gorgeous baby there!"

"You think she's gorgeous!" sniffed Mrs. Costanza. "Wait'll you see her pictures!"

YOU'RE NEVER TOO OLD TO LAUGH 45

An elderly woman climbed three flights of stairs, opened a carved mahogany door, and walked into an exotically furnished reception room. A gong sounded, and out of a cloud of incense appeared a beautiful Oriental brunette.

"Do you," she said softly, "wish to meet with his omnipotence, the wise, all-knowing, all-seeing guru, Maharishi Naru?"

"Yeah," said the gray-haired woman. "Tell Seymour, his grandmother is here from the Bronx!"

A woman is never as old
as her best friend says she is.

Shirley and Florence met at an AARP luncheon. "Darling," asked Shirley, "how's your granddaughter, the one married to the doctor?"

"Just got a divorce," replied Florence.

"Oh, my! Wasn't she married to a lawyer before him?"

"Yeah."

"But before, she divorced a dentist to marry the lawyer."

"That's right."

"And before the dentist, wasn't her first husband a CPA?" questioned Shirley.

"Yeah."

"Four professional men! Imagine, to get such pleasure from one grandchild!"

— — — —

"The undertakers did a real nice job on Miranda, didn't they?"

"Yeah. She used to be so wrinkled, her face would hold a two-day rain. 'Those aren't wrinkles, darling,' she used to say, 'I've just had a nap on the chenille spread.'"

> Some women grow old gracefully—
> others wear stretch pants.

———

To celebrate their thirtieth wedding anniversary, Mrs. Janos came home and presented her husband with a little monkey.

"Are you crazy or something?" shouted Mr. Janos. "Where the hell are we gonna keep a monkey?"

"Don't worry," she said, "he'll sleep right in the bed with us!"

"And what about the smell?"

"If I could stand it for thirty years—he'll get used to it also!"

———

A woman at the grave of her husband was wailing, "Oh, Herbert, it's four years since you've gone, but I still miss you!"

Just then Wessel passed by and saw the woman crying. " 'Scuse me," he said, "who are you mourning?"

"My husband," she said. "I miss him so much."

Wessel looked at the stone and then said, "Your husband? But it says on the gravestone, Sacred to the Memory of Rosemary Reyburn."

"Oh, yes, he put everything in my name."

Martha and Irene left their Leisure World homes and drove to town for lunch.

"Did you meet the new woman who moved in across the street?" asked Martha.

"I certainly did!" exclaimed Irene. "She couldn't stop complaining about her husband."

"Believe me, there's nothin' worse than a complaining wife," said Martha. "Now take me . . . my husband is a gambler, he drinks too much, he plays golf every day. A worse husband you never saw in your life! But do I ever say anything to anybody?"

————

TRIM FIGURES

What some Grannies do
when they tell their age.

Neala and Bridget, two widows, met in the laundry room of their Brooklyn apartment building. "Oh, my," exclaimed Neala. "Do you see what's goin' on in the Middle East, Bosnia, and Russia?"

"I don't see nothin'," said Bridget. "I live in the back."

Grandma Moskowitz was walking through Central Park with two little boys when she met a friend. "How old are your grandchildren?" asked the woman.

"The *doctor* is 5, and the *lawyer* is 7!" she answered proudly.

Four widowed golden girls were chatting while playing Mah-Jong. Each took a turn bragging about her children. When three of them had finished, Mrs. Weinstein began:

"Ladies," she said, "you don't know what it means to have a good son. My boy lives in a penthouse, and he built three rooms with a kitchen especially for me.

"He takes me out to dinner every night. We go to the theater three times a week. Last month he took me with him on vacation to the Virgin Islands. He don't do nothing without talking to me first.

"And ladies," added Mrs. Weinstein, "my son goes to a psychiatrist five times a week. And who do you think he spends the whole time talking about? Me!"

— — — —

"Darling, your stockings are wrinkled."
"But I'm not wearing any."

Mrs. Hurowitz had her portrait painted. When it was finished, the artist presented it to her. "How do you like it?" he asked.

"It's nice!" answered Mrs. Hurowitz. "But I want you should add a gold bracelet on each wrist. A pearl necklace, ruby earrings, an emerald tiara, and on each finger I want you to put a 20-carat diamond ring!"

"But," said the bewildered artist, "why do you want to ruin a good picture with all those gaudy trinkets?"

"My husband is running around with a girl young enough to be his granddaughter," explained Mrs. Hurowitz, "and when I die, I want her to go crazy looking for the jewelry!"

————

My grandma lived to 102. She didn't have wrinkles, she had pleats. There's one advantage to being 102. There's no peer pressure.

—Dennis Wolfberg

Stanley and Edith met at a community center singles' dance and within two weeks were married. They both felt it was a perfect match, for they were both 90 years old.

The first night of their honeymoon, they got into bed, and the old man squeezed Edith's hand. She squeezed back, and they fell asleep.

The second night, Stanley squeezed her hand again. Edith squeezed back, and they went right to sleep.

On the third night, Stanley once more squeezed his bride's hand. "Not tonight," said Edith, "I've got a headache!"

———

Audrey Wildman, Springfield's celebrated personal shopper, clicks with clients on this cutie:

Mrs. Thurlow called her 73-year-old neighbor, Mrs. Lance, to get some advice about what movie she should see with her husband that night. "How's the picture at the Regency One?" she asked. "Any good?"

"Don't go!" shouted the elderly Mrs. Lance. "We walked out in the middle. It was impossible to sit through it twice!"

Caroline: I hate to think of my youth.
　　Irma: What happened?
Caroline: Nothing!

————

Mrs. Levine and Mrs. Kahn, both widows, were sunning themselves on the roof of their Staten Island apartment building. They had known each other for over sixty years, but their everyday conversation still centered on dreams of having enormous wealth.

"Listen, if we was rich," said Mrs. Levine, "we would spend six months a year in Florida, six months in California, and six months in Europe."

"But," said Mrs. Kahn, "that makes eighteen months in one year."

"Ain't it grand what you could do with money?"

————

My grandmother's 90. She's dating. He's 93. It's going great. They never argue. They can't hear each other.

—Cathy Ladman

Mrs. Scarpelli was walking along the beach with her grandson, when suddenly from out of nowhere a wave came up and washed the 3-year-old boy out to sea.

"Oh, Lord," cried the woman, "if you'll just bring that boy back alive, I'll do anything! I'll be the best person. I'll give to the United Way. I'll go to church. Please, God! Send him back!"

At that moment, a wave washed the child back up on the sand, safe and sound. His grandmother looked at the boy and then up to the heavens.

"Okay," she exclaimed, "so where's his hat?"

————

A bride of 80 should not carry lilies. If she does, she must be careful to keep her eyes open during the ceremony.

—Phyllis Diller

Chapter Three

GLEEFUL GRUMBLERS

> *Growing old isn't
> so bad, especially when
> you consider the alternative.*
> —Maurice Chevalier

Reed, 94, and Dillon, 88, were the two oldest residents in an Orlando retirement residence. The doctors and staff believed both men continued to live only so they could provoke each other.

After an early lunch, the two were relaxing under a palm tree.

"Once I had a beard like yours," said Reed, "and when I saw how lousy I looked, I cut it off."

"I used to have a face like yours, too," said Dillon, "and when I saw how lousy it made me look, I grew a beard."

One day Reed and Dillon were sipping tea in the dining room. After a long silence, Reed said, "Life is like a bowl of sour cream."

"Why?" asked Dillon.

"How should I know? What am I, a philosopher?"

Livingston, 86, and Sardella, 78, were sitting on a Key West park bench. "My grandson gave me one of them VCRs," announced Livingston, "and last night I watched my first X-rated movie."

"How was it?" asked Sardella.

"I was so shocked, I could hardly sit through it the third time!"

————

Berkowitz was living it up at a Boca Raton seniors' dance, and he lost his wallet containing $600. "Excuse me," he announced, standing on a chair, "but I lost my wallet with $600 in it. To the person that finds it, I will give $50."

A voice from the rear shouted, "I'll give $75."

Mimi Marks, New Jersey's mirthful Saleswoman of the Year, cheers customers with this snippet of madcap merriment:

After thirty-eight years of marriage, Irma and Willard were still having their usual nightly fight. By 10 o'clock, Irma was tired and suddenly reversed her tactics. "In spite of all your faults, Willard, I've been in love with you since the first moment we met."

"Rubbish," sneered her husband. "If you had really loved me, you'd have married somebody else."

————

Reed and Dillon were relaxing on the patio of their Orlando retirement home.

"How old are you?" asked Reed.

"I don't know," replied Dillon.

"Take off your clothes. I'll tell you how old you are."

Dillon removed all his clothes. "Now," said Reed, "get down on your hands and knees."

Dillon followed instructions. "You're 94," said Reed.

"How'd you know?" asked Dillon.

"You told me yesterday!"

"Why're you lookin' at me like that?" asked Freeman.

"I'm trying to figure out one of the great mysteries of life," replied Miller. "How can that idiot who married your daughter be the father of the smartest grandchildren in the world?"

"I know you were a salesman for almost forty years. How did you handle insults?"

"Insults? Listen, I was selling in stores, on the road, door-to-door. I've been kicked out of places, my samples thrown on the floor, doors slammed in my face. But insulted? Never!"

Kendrick, 76, with the help of his cane, was shuffling slowly along Washington Avenue in Miami Beach.

A homeless beggar stopped him and asked, "Have you money for a cup of coffee, mister?"

"No," said Kendrick. "But don't worry about me, I'll get along just fine."

Three white-haired ladies playing cards poolside at the Eden Roc in Miami Beach were joined by a fourth.

"Sit down, darling!" said the leader of the group. "We're happy you should join us. We have certain rules while we're playing. First, we don't talk about our children. We've all got sons who are doctors and lawyers.

"Second, we don't talk about our grandchildren. We've all got gorgeous grandchildren.

"And third, we don't talk about sex! What was, was!"

Feinstein was crossing Collins Avenue in Miami Beach and was struck by a passing auto. Several passersby picked him up and laid him down on a bus bench.

A kindly silver-haired matron approached the injured man and said, "Are you comfortable?"

"Eh!" sighed Feinstein. "I make a living!"

No one is perfect, except the old
man who makes a perfect fool of himself.

The Kichlers were celebrating their thirtieth anniversary at the Coronado Hotel in San Diego with the biggest party held there in years. The husband sat at the head table totally depressed. His lawyer walked over to him and said, "What's wrong? Why do you look so unhappy?"

"Do you remember on my tenth anniversary," said Kichler, "I asked you what would happen if I murdered my wife?"

"Yes," answered the attorney. "I told you you'd get twenty years!"

"You see," said Kichler, "tonight, I'd be a free man!"

— — — —

"Things are terrible in the world today," grumbled Lawton.

"Be positive," said his friend. "If the stock market drops 80 points in one day, think of all the money you'll save on prune juice."

— — — —

The surest sign of growing old
is when you begin to regret
the sins you did not commit.

Reed: Do you believe in reincarnation?
Dillon: Yes. Because nobody could be as dumb as you are in one lifetime.

"I heard Pitkin passed away. What age was he?"
"I don't know exactly, but he was so old when he went to school they didn't have history."

Koenig was 78. His coffee-klatch buddy, Darnell, was a spry 84. One morning at the Seniors' Center, Koenig said, "Heard you got married."
"That's right," answered Darnell.
"Good lookin' woman?"
"Naw!"
"She a good cook?"
"No."
"Lotsa money?" asked Koenig.
"Heck, you're 84. If this woman ain't nice lookin' and she can't cook and she ain't rich, what did you marry her for?"
"She can drive at night!"

At a Clearwater retirement home, Hollis and Porter were talking on the porch. "Do you think there's as much sex and romance going on as there used to be?" asked Hollis.

"I guess so," nodded Porter, "except there's a new bunch doing it."

————

Reed: Do you believe it is possible to
        communicate with the dead?
Dillon: Yes, I can hear you distinctly.

————

Keeling, 81, Lyons, 83, and McKnight, 85, watched a pretty young blonde approaching.

"Gosh," said Keeling, "I'd sure like to take her out to dinner and the theater."

"I'd like to bite her on the ear," said Lyons.

"Well, I'd like to take her up to my room and kiss her," said McKnight. "And what's that other thing we used to do to girls?"

————

Growing old has one advantage:
you'll never have to do it over again.

YOU'RE NEVER TOO OLD TO LAUGH

Mrs. Fein and Mrs. Goldfarb, two gray-haired ladies, were sitting next to each other poolside at a Miami Beach hotel.

"Have you been through the menopause?" asked Mrs. Fein.

"The menopause?" answered Mrs. Goldfarb. "I haven't even been through the Fontainbleau yet."

Parnell was cooking hamburgers on the barbecue while visiting with his neighbor, Werner. They got around to comparing wives.

"My Cora is a saint," said Parnell. "She couldn't tell a lie to save her life."

"You lucky man," sighed Werner. "Eunice can tell a lie the minute I open my mouth."

"People tell me, 'Gee, you look good.' There are three ages of man: youth, middle age, and 'gee, you look good.' But I don't let old age bother me. There are three signs of old age. Loss of memory . . . I forgot the other two. My doctor said I look like a million dollars—green and wrinkled."

—Red Skelton

The Proctors were in their forty-sixth year of marriage. Mr. Proctor was not the type to compliment his wife, so she was surprised one evening when he called her an angel.

"Why did you call me an angel, dear?" asked Mrs. Proctor.

"Because you're always up in the air, you're continually harping on one thing or another, and you never have a damned thing to wear."

Oliver and Cory were walking home from their retirement community condominium Owners' Association meeting.

"I don't understand," said Oliver, "why you're always so darned dogmatic. You never seem to be able to see another person's point of view."

"That's ridiculous!" said Cory. "I tolerate all opinions—even stupid ones like yours."

What's all the big fuss about them birth control pills, like it was something new?

We had the same thing fifty years ago—only it was called army coffee.

The main conversation at most retirement communities is health. Ballock and Crawford were walking home from their computer class at Sun City.

"I just had my annual medical checkup, and my low blood pressure is lower than ever," announced Ballock.

"How bad is it?" asked Crawford.

"Well, if I cut myself, I have to do fifteen push-ups to start bleeding."

— — — —

Reed: This jug was made by a real Indian.
Dillon: But it says here it's made in Cleveland, Ohio.
Reed: What's the matter, you never heard of the Cleveland Indians?

Carlson, 67, and Boyle, 69, were having an early morning cappuccino at a San Diego coffee shop.

"You know," said Carlson, "this Sharon Stone, what does everyone see in her? Take away her hair, her lips, her eyes, and her figure, and what have you got?"

"My wife," said Boyle.

———

Hoffman, 76, and Grubb, 73, were playing chess.

"What's taking you so long to move?" asked Hoffman.

"I got a terrible headache today," said Grubb.

"Ah, headaches are all in your mind."

———

Watson, a 66-year-old Tampa stockbroker, was pouring his heart out to a friend.

"I'm nuts about this girl," he said. "Do you think I'd have a better chance of marrying her if I tell her I'm 50?"

"I think you'd have a better chance if you tell her you're 80."

"Do you think a father of 40 should get married again?"

"Never! That's more than enough children for any man!"

Rice and Kersh were relaxing on Miami Beach.

"My timing is terrible," grumbled Rice.

"What do you mean?" said Kersh.

"Just when the sexual revolution arrived, I ran out of ammunition."

Callahan and Porterfield were having lunch in a Boston sandwich shop.

"I thought your grandson was going to be an ear specialist," said Porterfield. "Now I understand you talked him into becoming a dentist."

"Not really," answered Callahan. "I just pointed out to him that people have thirty-two teeth and only two ears."

Reed: How do you feel today?
Dillon: I've got so many aches and pains that if a new one comes today, it will be at least two weeks before I can worry about it.

————

"Has going to that shrink helped you any?"
"Absolutely. I used to be terribly conceited, but my psychiatrist straightened me out. Now I'm one of the nicest guys in the state of Arizona."

————

You're never too old to learn—
but that's no reason to keep putting it off.

————

"Grandma," said Jennifer, "I want you to come to the community center with me tonight. The speaker is a famous psychologist."
"What will he talk about?" asked her grandmother.
"The role of sex in marriage."
"I already gave."

YOU'RE NEVER TOO OLD TO LAUGH

DEL RAY BEACH DIALOGUE

Ruby: What's wrong with your hair, honey?
It looks like a wig.
Emma: You know something, it is a wig!
Ruby: How do you like that—you never
could tell!

————

Who shows me what's what?
Who never nags or sasses?
Who clears my fuzzy thoughts?
My reading glasses.

————

OLD FOGY

One who disapproves of slacks for
women because woman's place is in the
home and not in men's pants.

"Hello, Grandma," shouted Sheldon over the phone. "I just won $10,000 in the state lottery! One of my tickets won!"

"Oh, that's wonderful!" said his grandmother. "But what did you mean, 'one of my tickets'?"

"I bought four, and one of them won."

"Dummy! Why did you need the other three?"

An old-timer is one who
can remember when the air was
clean and sex was dirty.

THE FIVE "B'S" OF OLD AGE

Balding, bursitis, bifocals,
bulges, and bunions.

Lefkowitz was a born grumbler. At 83, he still found nothing that pleased him. When Mike Piazza hit three home runs in one game, Lefkowitz commented, "It was okay." When they landed on the moon, the old man could only say, "Very nice."

One night his wife dragged him to the circus. Lefkowitz sneered at act after act. Finally the main attraction came on. A man tiptoed out on a thin wire, balanced one candle on his nose and another on his left foot. Then he put a violin under his chin, and suspended 200 feet in the air on one foot above a gasping crowd, he began to play the overture from *Carmen*.

"What do you think of that?" asked his wife.

"So," said Lefkowitz. "An Itzhak Perlman he ain't."

————

You know you've entered the
golden age when the silver in your
hair has turned to lead in your pants.

Noriko Stern, Florida's fun-filled flower of the Orient, entertains friends with this dash of frivolity:

Dr. Escobar entered the private room of a Miami hospital and spoke to his patient.

"Mr. Harrison, even though you are a very sick man, I think I'll be able to pull you through."

"Doctor, if you do that, when I get well I'll donate $500,000 for your new hospital."

Months later the MD met his former patient. "How do you feel?" he asked.

"Wonderful, Doctor, fine, never better."

"I've been meaning to speak to you," said Escobar, "about the money for the new hospital."

"Money? What are you talking about, Doctor?" grumbled Harrison.

"You said that if you got well, you would contribute $500,000 to the hospital."

"I said that?" asked the patient. "That just shows how sick I was."

There's no fool like an old fool—
you just can't beat experience.

YOU'RE NEVER TOO OLD TO LAUGH 73

The new neighbor joined the bridge group for the first time, and all the ladies gaped at the huge diamond she wore. "It's the third most famous diamond in the world," she told the women. "First is the Cullian diamond, then the Hope diamond, and then this one—the Schmulowitz diamond."

"It's beautiful!" said Mrs. Rowe. "You're so lucky!"

"Not so lucky," sighed the newcomer. "Unfortunately, with the famous Schmulowitz diamond, I am afflicted with the famous Schmulowitz curse."

"What's that?" asked Mrs. Rowe.

"Mister Schmulowitz," said the woman.

When Trombley had reached the age of 65, he suddenly began chasing the babes. A neighbor brought his behavior to the attention of his wife. "Whatta you gonna do about it?" she asked.

"Who cares?" said Mrs. Trombley. "Let him chase girls! Dogs chase cars, but when they catch them—they can't drive!"

O'Brien took his Social Security check down to the bank to deposit it. As he stood and waited in the long line, he inadvertently began to nervously fold and unfold his check.

It finally came his turn at the teller's window. As O'Brien handed the teller a ruffled government check, she said, "Sir, can't you read this check? It says, 'Do not fold, spindle, or mutilate.'"

"So?" replied the customer.

"Well," said the teller, "you shouldn't do that. The government doesn't like it."

Looking her straight in the eye, he replied, "Well, the government does a lot of things I don't like, too!"

––––

Old age is that time in life when
the little gray-haired lady you help
across the street is your own wife.

Chapter Four

GROOVY GRANDADS

You can't help getting older, but you don't have to get old.
—George Burns

Grandpa Palmer was caught unprepared by the Minnesota cold spell last winter and complained to his grandson that he hadn't been able to sleep.

"Did your teeth chatter, Grandpa?"

"Dunno," he replied. "We didn't sleep together."

————

Fuller was in good shape, even though he was 90 years of age. Knowing that he was a former bodybuilder and a great athlete, a newspaper reporter asked, "What exercise do you do to stay fit?"

"My boy," replied the old man, "when you're pushing 90, that's the only exercise you need!"

A reporter was interviewing Nevell on his ninety-ninth birthday. "I certainly hope I can come back next year and see you reach the century mark," he said.

"Can't see any reason why not, young feller," replied Nevell. "You look healthy enough to me!"

Moore, 76: When I die, I hope it is in a hurry. I'd be satisfied to die in the crash of a speeding car.

Sloan, 84: I think it would be better to die in a plane crash.

Noyes, 95: I've got a better idea—I'd rather die from smoke inhalation from blowing out one hundred candles on my birthday cake.

Rich old Parker lay dying. He gave instructions to have his body cremated after death, and the ashes placed in an envelope and sent to the IRS with a note: "Now you have everything."

A young insurance salesman was trying to sell 95-year-old Osborne an insurance policy. "I'm not interested," said the old gentleman. "I don't plan to live that long."

"Well," said the salesman, "we have a special today on a ten-year policy."

"No," said Osborne, "I don't plan to live that long."

"My company has just issued a brand new five-year policy, and you'll be the first one to receive this offer."

The 95-year-old Osborne said, "You don't seem to understand. At my age, I don't even buy green bananas!"

― ― ― ―

Binker and his buddy, Cameron, were taking their afternoon stroll on the Asbury Park boardwalk. "How you been doin' with the ladies lately?" asked Binker.

"Oh, I tried to date that good-looking widow who's a waitress down at Denny's," said Cameron.

"How's it goin'?"

"Aw, she only likes men who put their cards on the table: Visa, Diner's Club, American Express . . ."

Grandpa Godwin was a farmer. He didn't claim to know much, but he always had a good crop. Once a student from the state agricultural college came out to see him.

"Your methods of cultivation are hopelessly out of date," said the young man. "Why, I'd be surprised if you get ten pounds of apples off that tree."

"So would I," responded Godwin. "It's a pear tree!"

Jaeger finally invested in a hearing aid after becoming virtually deaf. It was one of those invisible kinds.

"How do you like your new hearing aid?" asked his doctor.

"I like it great. I've heard sounds in the last few weeks that I didn't know existed."

"Well, how does your family like your hearing aid?"

"Nobody in my family knows I have it yet. And I'm having a great time! I've changed my will three times in the last two months!"

McPherson hated to part with a penny, but he was becoming increasingly hard of hearing. The old man decided a hearing aid was too expensive, so he wrapped an ordinary piece of wire around his ear. A friend asked him, "Do you hear better now with that wire around your ear?"

"Not a bit, but everybody talks louder."

On his one hundredth birthday, Grandpa was asked by his grandson, "Where would you say the greatest progress has been made during your lifetime?"

The old man laughed. "From the things they now call good clean fun, I'd say when the straight and narrow path was widened to a twelve-lane highway."

Mrs. Kleiber, 78, loved concerts. Husband, Hank, 79, hated them. One night he did everything to be late for a performance of senior musicians.

They finally arrived at 10 o'clock. The orchestra was in the middle of an opus. Mrs. Kleiber looked at the program and said, "We are now into Beethoven's Ninth Symphony."

"Oh, boy," said her husband, "am I glad I missed the other eight."

OLD-TIMER

One who can remember when a
"bureau" was a piece of furniture.

A wealthy widower and his daughter were traveling to Europe on the *Queen Elizabeth II*. One evening after dinner, they were strolling along the Promenade Deck when the girl fell overboard. Feldman, age 73, hit the water and saved her. After the two were brought back aboard the ship, the father threw his arms around Feldman.

"You saved my daughter's life," he exclaimed. "I'm a rich man. I'll give you anything. Ask me for whatever you want!"

"Just answer me one question!" said Feldman. "Who pushed me?"

An inquiring reporter from the *Cleveland Plain Dealer* stopped a well-dressed senior on Woodward Avenue and asked, "Are you against sin?"

"Of course I'm against sin," he replied. "I'm against anything I'm too old to enjoy."

————

Mr. and Mrs. Bernstein were having a sixtieth wedding anniversary party at a Long Island restaurant. A TV nightly news crew was there to record the event. "How old is your wife?" asked the newscaster.

"She's 87," said Bernstein, "and God willing, she'll live to be 100!"

"And how old are you?" inquired the reporter.

"I'm 87, too," answered the octogenarian, "and God willing, I'll live to be 101!"

"But why would you want to live a year longer than your wife?"

"To tell you the truth," said Bernstein, "I'd like to have at least one year of peace!"

————

Man: Hello, Sally. Do you still love me?
Woman: Sally? My name is Laurette.
Man: I'm so sorry—I keep thinking this is Tuesday.

My grandfather's a little forgetful, but he likes to give me advice. One day he took me aside and left me there.

—Ron Richards

Goldstein, on his deathbed, was surrounded by his children. "Don't worry, Papa, we'll have a big funeral," declared his eldest son. "There'll be one hundred limousines, ten cars with flowers."

"We don't need all that," interrupted Goldstein's second son. "Fifty limos and five cars with flowers is more than enough!"

"Whatta ya makin' such a big deal," said the dying man's youngest son. "We don't need any flowers. We'll just have the immediate family. Two cars is enough!"

Suddenly Goldstein raised himself up and said, "Listen, boys! Just hand me my pants—I'll walk to the cemetery!"

An eccentric old fellow named Roffin
Once remarked in a bad fit of coughin',
  "It isn't the cough
  That carries you off.
It's the coffin they carry you off in."

I'll tell you how to stay young—hang around with older people.

—Bob Hope

Al Jolson used to tell this one about his father:
"I bought my dad an overcoat that cost a couple a hundred bucks. It was beautiful! But I knew the old guy'd say $200 was too much to spend for the coat. So I told him it only cost $10.

"Three weeks later, he phoned me backstage at the Winter Garden, and I said, 'Pop, did you get the coat I sent you?'

"He said, 'Yeah, that overcoat was some buy for $10. I sold it to your uncle Max for $20. Send me a dozen more!'"

When George Gershwin became successful, he brought his immigrant father to California. One day the senior Gershwin, who spoke English with a heavy accent, was stopped by a motorcycle cop for speeding.

"You can't give me a ticket," declared Grampa Gershwin. "My son is *Chudge* Gershwin!"

"Okay," said the officer, "I'll just give you a warning this time." And as he drove away, he shouted, "Give my regards to the judge."

Compton was 92. He and his longtime friend Tyree, 88, were sitting on a bench in a St. Louis park playing checkers.

After the third game, Compton said, "I got a big announcement to make."

"What's that?" asked his friend.

"I'm getting married. I've been alone too long."

"Who you going to marry?" said Tyree.

"Kristie, the dietician down at the Seniors' Center."

"Kristie is 19 years old. Ninety-two and 19 are going to get married?"

"Why not? She's exactly the age of my first wife when I married *her!*"

YOU'RE NEVER TOO OLD TO LAUGH 85

Barbara Oman, Carmel's champion organic gardener, gets giggles with this gleeful gem:

Grandpa Brennan didn't know much about plants. One day his neighbor, Mrs. Matson, was showing him through her new greenhouse.

"This plant belongs to the begonia family," she explained.

"Oh," gushed Grandpa, "how nice of you to look after it while they're away."

— — — —

The Weltmans married off their last daughter and decided to sell their house and move into a furnished apartment.

Weltman showed his wife the apartment he rented.

"I don't like it," she said.

"Why not?" asked Weltman.

"There's no curtains in the bathroom," she complained. "Every time I take a bath, the neighbors'll be able to see me in the nude!"

"Don't worry," said her husband, "when the neighbors see you in the nude, they'll buy the curtains."

On her deathbed, Eloise was giving final instructions to her husband.

"Robert, you've been so good to me all these years. I know you never even thought about another woman. Now that I'm going, I want you to marry again as soon as possible, and I want you to give your new wife all my expensive clothes."

"I can't do that, darling," he said. "You're a size 16 and she's only a 10!"

TELLTALE SIGNS OF AGE

Your mind makes promises your body can't keep.

You look forward to a dull evening.

Your knees buckle, and your belt won't.

You regret all those mistakes you made resisting temptation.

Your back goes out more than you do.

You turn out the lights to save money, not to get romantic.

You feel like it's the morning after, but you didn't do anything the night before.

Old man Teitleberg lay on his deathbed for months and finally passed away.

Two weeks later, the relatives gathered like vultures to hear the reading of the will.

The lawyer tore open an envelope, drew out a piece of paper, and read:

" 'Being of sound mind, I spent every dime before I died.' "

————

It takes about ten years
to get used to how old you are.

————

Old Holloway was very proud of this year's corn crop. He had heard that the best way to freeze corn was in condoms. An ear of corn to each rubber.

On Thursday, he purchased a dozen to try them out. It worked so well that on Friday he bought two dozen more.

He decided to put more in the freezer. On Saturday he went back for another three dozen condoms, but the store was completely sold out.

"Gee," sighed the young girl who had waited on him for all of his purchases, "I hope we haven't spoiled your Saturday night for you."

Great-grandpa Gregory had lived a good life until 94, when he finally died. Several years later, Emil, his boyhood friend, joined Gregory in heaven and found him seated on a fluffy pink cloud, with a pretty young blonde at his knees.

"Wonderful," said Emil. "I'm so happy to see you've received the reward you deserve."

"She isn't my reward," sighed the old man. "I'm her punishment."

— — — —

Bernard Blumberg, the worldly wise voyager, breaks up fellow travelers with this bauble:

Barnes and Hart were sitting on a Pittsburgh park bench. "I'll tell you the truth," said Barnes, "I'm afraid to fly. Those airplanes ain't too safe!"

"Don't be a baby," said Hart. "Didn't you read last week there was a big train crash and three hundred people were killed!"

"Three hundred killed on a train—what happened?"

"An airplane fell on it!"

There was an old man named MacLeith
Who sat on his set of false teeth.
  He cried with a start,
  "Oh, Lord, bless my heart!
I've bitten myself underneath!"

Old age does have some advantages. Not only can you sing while you shower, you can sing while you brush your teeth.

—George Jessel

Ralph Vissell, San Francisco's millionaire man-about-town, makes merry with this smidgen of satire:

Professor Prendville was going to Africa on a research trip and put a classified ad in the newspaper:

WANTED
*A man who speaks at least five
languages, who loves to travel,
and knows how to use a gun.*

The next day, Bleiberg, 79, applied.

"Do you love to travel?" asked Prendville.

"I hate traveling," said Bleiberg. "Boats make me seasick, planes I wouldn't get on, and trains are the worst of them all."

"But you are a linguist," continued the professor. "Of course, I presume you speak Urdu, Arabic, Greek—"

"Sorry," interrupted the old man. "I don't know hardly any foreign languages."

"Well, you can use firearms?" persisted the professor.

"No, I'm afraid from guns."

"Then what the devil did you come here for?"

"I saw your ad," said Bleiberg, "and I just came to tell you that on me you shouldn't depend."

A wealthy Gross Pointe socialite was talking to Dawkins to see if she could hire him to cut her grass. They had difficulty negotiating a fee, so finally she said, "I'll tell you what. Let's give it a trial—you come to work for me on Tuesday, and I'll pay you what you're worth."

"That don't make no sense!" said Dawkins. "I get more than that from Social Security."

Mrs. Hartley bought a new line of expensive cosmetics guaranteed to make her look years younger. After applying the "miracle" products for over an hour, she asked the widower Lynch, "Darling, honestly, what age would you say I am?"

Looking her over carefully, he replied, "Judging from your skin, 20; your hair, 18; and your figure, 25."

"Oh, you flatterer!" she gushed.

"Wait a minute! I haven't added them up yet."

At my age, when I order a three-minute egg, they ask for the money up front.
—Milton Berle

Cloyd and Royce were visiting in front of a small-town general store.

"Doctor gave me some pills yesterday to improve my memory," said Cloyd.

"So?" answered Royce.

"So, I forgot to take them."

————

"How old do you think Cartwright is?"

"He's so old, his blood type was discontinued."

————

An elderly Missouri farmer, who had little patience with children, finally surrendered to the charms of his attractive young housekeeper, the mother of a 10-year-old brat.

Soon after the marriage, she went to Kansas City to do some shopping. Upon her return, she asked her son how he got along with his new father.

"Okay," said the youngster. "Every morning he took me out on the lake in a rowboat and let me swim back."

"Heavens, that's a long distance to swim!"

"Oh, I made it all right," said the boy. "Only trouble I had was getting out of the burlap bag."

Nolan and his wife were driving home from a seniors' social at Arizona's Sun City.

"You didn't laugh at Tooley's joke," said Mrs. Nolan. "I thought it was a good one."

"It was a good one," replied Nolan, "but I can't stand Tooley. I'll laugh when I get home."

Gabriella and Tony went to visit her father for the first time in a retirement home. They spotted a white-haired fellow hobbling along with a cane. "S'cuse me," said Tony, "we're looking for Raymond Keegan."

"Wha-a-a-t?" asked the elderly gent, cupping his hand to his ear.

"We want to see Ray Keegan."

"Who?"

"Ray Keegan!" shouted Tony.

"That's me."

"No," said Gabriella, "the other Ray Keegan."

"Oh, the old man! He's in room 226."

"Lieberman must be well on in age."

"Yes. Poor man. He's so old he gets winded playing checkers!"

Betty Poulos, Hanna, Wyoming's, sparkling socialite, gets belly laughs at the Nugget Bar with this beaut:

The widow Elford invited a date to a Cheyenne country club party. She sat in a corner, eyeing her escort with great disapproval. "That's the fourth time you've gone back for more roast beef and lobster salad, Harley," she said. "Doesn't it embarrass you at all?"

"Why should it?" said the old man. "I keep telling them I'm getting it for you."

Deming, 88, and Fincher, 89, were fighting feeblemindedness. As they trudged along Chicago's Lake Shore Drive, it suddenly began to rain.

"Open your umbrella!" said Deming.

"My umbrella ain't worth a damn," said Fincher. "It's full of holes."

"Holes? Then why did you bring it?"

"Did I know it was gonna rain?"

> No man ever knows true happiness until he has a complete set of false teeth and has lost all interest in the opposite sex.
> —Lord Rosebury

> Nothing gives a man
> More of a chill,
> Than to have his grandkids ask
> If he's made out his will.

Grandpa McCormick opened his eyes and discovered a woman in a white uniform staring at him. "Where am I?" he asked.

"You were in an auto accident, and you've been unconscious for six days!" replied the nurse. "You're in the best hospital with the best doctors, getting the finest medical care."

"I'm here six days?" asked the senior. "No wonder I'm hungry! Could you bring me some corned beef and cabbage?"

"No, you're being fed rectally," said the woman. "If you reach under and behind you, you'll feel a large tube."

"If this is the best hospital, with the best doctors, and the finest medical care, you must have more tubes."

"Yes, Mr. McCormick, we have plenty. Why?"

"Tomorrow, bring two more tubes, I'd like you and the doctor to join me for lunch!"

Chapter Five

GENIAL GRIPERS

> *It's bad to suppress laughter. It goes back down and spreads to the hips.*
> —Fred Allen

"Doctor, I'm suffering from bad memory. I've no sooner said something than I've forgotten what I've said."

"And how long has this been going on?"

"How long has what been going on?"

"Doc, I've got a bad problem," complained the bent-over, silvery-haired old man. "I'm 91 years old and still chasing women."

"What's wrong with that, old fellow?" asked the doctor.

"Well," he sighed, "I chase 'em, but I can't remember why."

"Doctor, I don't know what's wrong with me. Every morning at 7 o'clock, I have a bowel movement."

"What's wrong with that?"

"I don't get out of bed until 9 o'clock."

————

Carver lay completely bandaged in his hospital room. He had to be fed rectally through a tube. One morning as a special treat, the nurse gave him coffee. Carver began screaming through his bandages and tried to shove the tube away.

"What's the matter?" asked the nurse. "Too hot?"

"No, No!" he moaned, "too much sugar!"

————

Whitman was sitting in a doctor's waiting room. "I hope I'm sick. I hope I'm sick."

"Hey," said the man across from him, "why do you keep saying that you hope you're sick?"

"I'd hate to be well and feel like this!" he griped.

Old Mrs. Tachaloni went to a physician and complained of constipation.

"Do you do anything about it?" asked the MD.

"Of course I do. I sit on the toilet for three hours every day."

"No, no, I don't mean that. I mean do you take anything?"

"Of course," said the elderly woman. "I take along my knitting."

Doctor: Shall I give your wife a local anesthetic?
Wealthy Texan: No. I'm rich. Give her the best. Give her something imported!

"Doctor, I dreamt five nights in a row that Julia Roberts was trying to hug me and kiss me, and I kept pushing her away."

"Well, what do you want me to do?"

"I want you to break my arms."

"Are you troubled with dirty thoughts?"

"To tell you the truth, Doctor, I rather enjoy them."

————

Old Doc Willingham passed away. A group of his friends decided to collect some money to give him a nice funeral. Their collection was not going well until they called on Ramsey, an eccentric elderly rancher.

"How much were you hoping for from me?" he demanded.

"$100 to bury the doctor," suggested their leader.

Ramsey pulled out his wallet and said, "Here's $1,000. Bury ten of 'em."

————

Young Dr. Dietrich completed an examination of an elderly man.

"Tell me," asked the MD, "do you suffer from arthritis?"

"Of course!" snarled the senior. "What the hell else can I do with it?"

The well-known surgeon wanted to establish some rapport with a senior to whom he had given an estimate on a heart operation. "Your grandkids are no wilder than any of us when we were the same age," schmoozed the surgeon. "Why, when I was a boy, I had a great ambition to be a pirate."

"You're lucky," said the patient, "not every man gets to be what he wants!"

Rodriguez boarded a San Antonio bus, his hands outstretched and held apart in a circle from his body. He said to the driver, "Take the dollar from this right pocket and place a transfer in the left pocket." His hands were still held out in that rigid position.

"What's the matter, you paralyzed?" asked the driver.

"No, señor. The doctor order a bedpan for my wife, and I no want to lose the measurement."

Everybody wants to live a
long time, but nobody wants to get old.

"How do you feel?" asked the doctor. "Sort of sluggish?"

"Sluggish?" answered the patient. "Say, if I felt that good I wouldn't even be here!"

A nifty ol' fella from Weston
Has 50 feet of intestine;
   Though a renowned success
   In the medical press
It isn't much good for digestin'.

"I just had a prostate operation, and the doctor left a sponge in me."

"Got any pain?"

"No, but boy, do I ever get thirsty!"

Doctor: I don't like the looks of your husband.
Wife: I don't either, but he's good to the grandchildren.

Harper the aging hypochondriac began sobbing before a doctor. "I'm sure I've got a liver disease, and I'm gonna die from it."

"Ridiculous," said the MD. "You'd never know if you had the disease or not. With that ailment there's no discomfort of any kind."

"Right," said Harper, "those are my exact symptoms."

Dr. Erhardt examined a new patient very carefully. After studying the X-rays, he said to the elderly man, "Could you pay for an operation if I told you it was necessary?"

"Would you find one necessary if I told you I couldn't pay for it?"

Dr. Landers was very pleased with his patient's progress. "You're coughing more easily this morning."

"Well, I ought to. I've been practicing all night."

Henderson, 77, complained to his doctor, "I got insomnia real bad."

"Insomnia," said the physician, "is insomnia. How bad can it be? What do you mean, 'real bad insomnia'?"

"I got it real bad," said the patient. "I can't even sleep when it's time to get up!"

————

Thurleen, a 76-year-old widow, visited Dr. Hatch and complained about her memory. After an examination, the MD asked, "Do you have difficulty making up your mind?"

"Well, yes and no."

————

Dr. Woodruff appeared for his nightly visit at the home of a sick man. "Have you been following my instructions closely?" he asked the wife.

"Yes. I gave him juice, just like you said. Battery juices."

"*Battery* juices!" barked the MD. "Good Lord! He'll die."

"No, he won't," she replied. "He has a cold. He can't taste a thing."

A man is really getting old
And lost his zip and snap,
When a pretty girl gets on his nerves
Instead of on his lap.

― ― ― ―

Bostwick went to Dr. Gordon, the optician, and announced, "I want to get my eyes tested for a pair of glasses."

Gordon placed him in front of a card and asked, "Can you read that plainly?"

"No, I can't," replied Bostwick.

The doctor moved the card closer and asked, "Can you read it now?"

"No, I can't."

Gordon took the card and pushed it right under his nose. "Well, can you read it now?"

"No," said Bostwick. "I never learned to read yet."

"That pain in your leg is caused by old age," the doctor told his elderly patient.

"That can't be," said the man. "The other leg's the same age, and it doesn't hurt a bit."

The slick con man was selling a magic elixir guaranteed to make humans live forever. A crowd of older people outside the Albertson supermarket listened in awed silence.

"Take a good look at me," said the con man. "Feast your eyes on a man who is 250 years old."

Washburn, 77, walked over to the con man's young assistant and asked, "Is he really that old?"

"I don't know," said the assistant. "I've only been working for him for seventy-five years."

The old man growled, "Where the heck are my glasses?"

"On your nose," said his wife.

"Be more specific!"

"My wife always lies about her age."

"My Jenny never lies about her age. She just tells people she's as old as I am. Then she lies about *my* age."

"Doctor, I'm 87 years of age. I am getting married Saturday to a real pretty 19-year-old girl."

"You must be crazy. That could be fatal."

"Well, if she dies, she dies!"

"What about my bill?" asked Dr. Carleson.

"I can't pay it," said Boonton, "but if you'll take me down to your cellar, I'll show you how to fix your meter so you can cheat the gas company."

Gridley and Melburn, two elderly, bored, long-term hospital patients, swiped the diagnosis cards from the nurses' station for a quick game. It was draw poker. There was a lot of money bet on one particular hand, and all the loot ended up on the table.

"Sorry. I guess I win," offered Gridley. "I have gallstones and three tonsillectomies."

"Not so fast," said Melburn. "I've got four enemas. I win the pot."

― ― ― ―

Farley, age 79, went to Dr. Stanton and complained that his hearing was slowly deteriorating. After a long and careful examination, Stanton advised him to stop drinking any alcoholic beverages.

Farley followed the physician's advice and at his next appointment informed the MD that his hearing had in fact shown an immediate improvement.

However, three months later, the senior went back to the medic and reported sorrowfully that he had become completely deaf.

"You haven't started drinking again, have you?" demanded the doctor.

"Yes," admitted the old man. "I'm afraid I have."

"Why?"

"I suppose it was because I liked what I was drinking much more than what I was hearing."

Old age is the period when you begin to smile at things you used to laugh at.

"Mrs. Vardell, this may sting just a little," said the doctor, as he prepared the syringe of antibiotic and stepped forward to administer it.

The patient suddenly screamed in agonizing pain and crumpled to the floor.

The physician picked her up and exclaimed, "Mrs. Vardell, this is ridiculous. I haven't even inserted the needle yet!"

"No," she said, "but you stepped on my ingrown toenail!"

A shy little old lady went to Dr. Beeman for the first time. "What can I do for you?" he asked.

"To tell you the truth, Doctor, I have aches and pains everyplace."

"Well, then, please remove all your clothes, and I'll examine you."

"What! You want I should take off all my clothes?"

"Of course."

"You first!"

"I believe time heals everything."
"Yeah? You never tried sitting it out in my doctor's waiting room."

"Sure is rough trying to make ends meet each month just on a little Social Security."
"There is one advantage to being poor—a doctor will cure you faster."

"Mrs. Mulroy, did you take your husband's temperature this morning the way I asked you to?"
"Yes, doctor. I placed a barometer on his chest. It said 'very dry,' so I gave him a pint of beer, and he went to play golf."

At an AARP meeting, a 96-year-old woman showed up sporting a sweatshirt that said:
*It's hard to be nostalgic
when you can't remember
a damn thing.*

Peacock went to see a doctor and complained about a boil on his neck.

"It is being caused by a bad tooth," the doctor assured him.

Peacock took out both his denture plates, laid them on the table, and said: "You point out which tooth it is, Doc, and I'll knock it off right away."

― ― ― ―

Mrs. Rickman was very jealous because all her neighbors were getting things free from Medicare. One had new teeth, another had new glasses, and when the woman next door got a free hearing aid, it was the last straw.

She went to the doctor and said, "I'd like you to cut a hole in my stomach."

"Are you serious?"

"Yes, I want you to make a hole and fit a piece of glass in it."

"Mrs. Rickman, I'll prescribe some tranquilizers."

"I don't want tranquilizers!"

"What do you want then?"

"I just told you—a womb with a view!"

Septuagenarian comedian Richard Carter counters the assault of time with blunt irreverence:

"There's a lot to be said about Alzheimer's disease. You get to wake up every morning and meet new people.

"And you can save a lot of money by forgetting. My grandson said, 'Grandpa, you forgot my birthday.' I said, 'Who the hell are you?' "

––––

Eighty-two-year-old McCready was recovering nicely. Each day from his hospital bed, he pinched the nurse's behind and made lewd remarks.

"With your mind," she scolded, "you should be living in a bordello."

"At these prices," said the old man, "I could afford to."

––––

Another sign of age is when you feel
like the morning after the night before
—and you haven't even been anywhere.

It's too bad we can't use,
Said a man, 87.
Our tombstone inscriptions
As passports to heaven!

Mrs. Schecter visited Dr. Wade, the gynecologist, to complain about her ailments.

"Yesterday I went to the bathroom in the morning," she began, "and I heard a plink-plink in the toilet. When I looked down, the water was full of pennies."

"I see," offered the MD.

"That afternoon I went again, and there were nickels in the bowl."

"Uh-huh."

"Last night there were dimes, and this morning, doctor, there were quarters!" griped the woman. "You've got to tell me what's wrong."

"It's nothing to be scared about. You're simply going through your change."

Chapter Six

GIGGLING GRANDCRITTERS

It's easy to understand why God rested on the seventh day.

He didn't have grandkids.

"My goodness!" said Grandma Gertrude. "You've put on some weight, haven't you?"

"I hope so," retorted Zachary. "I weighed only 8 pounds when I was born."

Young Mark was sitting at the breakfast table when his grandfather barged into the kitchen and shouted, "Damn it!"

"What's the matter, Dad?" asked Mark's mother.

"This brush is no good," said the senior. "I can't shave with it."

"That's funny," said the boy. "It was okay this morning when I washed my bike with it."

Betty Brookes, Ohio's favorite globe-trotter, loves this timeless titillater:

When Jonathan arrived at his grandmother's house in the country, she gave him permission to look at the lake nearby but not to go in the water.

An hour later, Jonathan showed up at the house with his long red hair drenched. Grandma demanded an explanation, "I fell in," he explained.

"Then how come your clothes are dry?" asked his grandmother.

"I took them off," replied the boy. "I had a feeling I was going to fall in."

"Be a good boy, Eugene, and eat your spinach," urged the boy's grandmother. "It will put color in your cheeks."

"But, Grandma," he whined, "who needs green cheeks!"

Grandmother: Another bite like that, and you will have to leave the table.

Hungry boy: Another bite like that, and I'll be through.

YOU'RE NEVER TOO OLD TO LAUGH 117

Grandma Goodman and her little grandson arrived early at Disneyland. For several hours, they had a lot of fun, but it was exhausting for Grandma. About noon, she sat down to rest. Realizing it was lunchtime, she handed him some money.

"Take this and get somethin' to eat," she instructed. "But first, tell me what you're going to buy."

"Oh, boy, $20!" exclaimed the youngster. "I'm gonna buy popcorn, peanuts, hot dogs, a caramel apple, ice cream, Hershey bars, and . . . and . . . and . . ." He saw Grandma glaring at him and added, "and a green vegetable!"

Prudence proudly introduced her grandson to a charity committee friend. "This is my grandson, Todd, Mrs. Foster. Isn't he a bright little boy?"

The youngster, quite accustomed to being shown off in public, purred, "What was that clever thing I said yesterday, Grandmama?"

Most grandchildren hate to
begin a meal on an empty stomach.

"I'm going to make a strawberry shortcake for dinner," said Grandma Thornley.

"Can I help?" asked little Karen.

"Sure," said the woman. "You can wash the strawberries."

Mrs. Thornley gave Karen a pan of strawberries. Soon she called, "Are you washing all the strawberries? Are you doing a good job?"

"Oh, yes, Nana," said the youngster. "I'm using lots of soap!"

————

Dinner's defrosting,
Grandma's not;
Today's her birthday,
And Gramps forgot.

————

Mrs. Gordon asked her grandson, "Why are you holding up that slice of bread?"

"I'd like to propose a toast!" said the boy.

If you think practice makes perfect, you don't have a grandchild taking piano lessons.

Joyce Wolf, the celebrated Santa Rosa sculptress, savors this smile-getter:

Mrs. Turner had been baking oatmeal cookies. While she had a batch in the oven, the phone rang in the den. After a long conversation, she remembered her cookies and rushed to the kitchen to find it filled with smoke.

Quickly she removed the charred cookie sheets and sat down, utterly depressed. Suddenly she felt the soft hand of her 3-year-old granddaughter. "Don't feel bad, Gamma," said the tiny voice. "That's the best-smelling smoke you ever made."

Ten-year-old Rocco was going to sell soft drinks at the park and asked his grandfather if he could borrow a wrench.

"You mean a bottle opener, don't you?" suggested his grandfather.

"No," said the boy, "a wrench. First I've got to turn off the water at all the drinking fountains."

If Gramps can remember so many jokes
With all the details that mold them,
Why can't he recall, with equal skill,
How many times he's told them?

————

Carolee Gluek entertained her tablemates aboard a Crystal Harmony cruise to Alaska with this nifty nugget of nonsense:

Grandma Charlotte, napping soundly on the living room couch, was suddenly awakened by her 6-year-old granddaughter, Melissa. The child was running her fingers across her grandmother's face.

"What in the world are you doing?" asked the startled woman.

"Daddy told me you can tell the age of a tree by counting the lines. I'm trying to figure out how old you are."

————

Olivia and Tiffany, two teenagers, were comparing grandmother notes. "My grandma is cool," offered Olivia, "and she's young, too."

"You're lucky," said Tiffany. "My grandmom is so old, at her birthday parties the candles cost more than the cake."

"Alfred," said his grandmother, "don't you know you are not supposed to eat with your knife?"

"I know, Grandma, but my fork leaks."

Grandpa Bernhard looked very different to Christina when he came on a recent visit. He had shaved off his big beard, and it was the first time she had seen him with a smooth, clean face.

"Oh, Grandpa!" exclaimed the child. "Whose head have you got on?"

Warren came home from school with two black eyes. "You've been fighting again," said his grandmother. "Why didn't you count to ten before getting angry, like I've always told you to do?"

"I did," said the boy, "but the other guy's grandmother told him to count up to five!"

The only things that children
wear out faster than shoes
are grandparents.

"Melvin," screamed his grandmother, "you've been fighting again, and this time you've lost all your teeth."

"No, I haven't, Gramma," protested the boy. "I got 'em right here in my pocket."

Visiting Grampa: If you're really good, Tyler, I'll give you this brand new one-dollar bill.

Tyler: Haven't you got a dirty old twenty?

Hector, age 5, was giving his grandmother every conceivable argument why he shouldn't go to school.

After telling him every reason why he should go to school, his grandmother finally added: "Hector, don't you know that if you didn't go to school, your grandfather would have to go to jail?"

"For how long?" replied the boy.

In spite of all their messin',
Grandchildren are a blessin'.

While his grandchildren were vacationing with him, Grandpa Daniels decided to teach the facts of life to David, the 10-year-old. He sat the boy down and, rather nervously, explained all about the bees and the flowers.

When he finished, Grandpa suggested that the boy pass on this information to his 8-year-old brother.

David went to his younger brother's room and said to him, "You know what married people do when they want to have kids? Grandpa says that bees and flowers do the same thing."

Dustin, the high school football star, was asked by his grandfather, "What is the first thing you notice about a girl?"

"Well," replied the teenager, "that all depends on which direction she's facing."

Grandchildren are not only a
comfort to a man when he reaches
old age, they help bring it on.

————

Mrs. Janos stood in line at the Safeway supermarket and turned to check on her small grandson. "What're you doing?" she demanded.
"Nuthin, Grandma," he replied.
"Well, quit it!" she snapped.

————

Donald's long-suffering parents deposited him at his grandmother's house for a two-week visit. The sweet old lady insisted that she was well able to handle the boy. The parents had their misgivings, and then they received his first letter:

Dear Mom and Pop,

It sure is nice here, and we're having lots of fun. This morning me and Grandma played cops and robbers, and she's gonna bake me lots of cookies as soon as I untie her.

Love,
Donald

The passing years
Sure make me ponder
Why Gramps gets gray
And Grandma gets blonder.

"You're always asking questions," said Perry's grandfather. "I'd like to know what would have happened if I'd asked as many questions when I was a boy."

"Maybe," said Perry, "you'd have been able to answer some of mine."

Little Julio: Grandpa, was you with Noah in the Ark?
Grandpa: I can't say I was.
Little Julio: Then how come you wasn't drowned?

"Carolyn, drink your milk like a good girl," ordered her mother. "It will make your teeth strong."

"Mama, if it's so good for the teeth," said the child taking a sip, "why don't you give my share to Grandma?"

No wonder it's so difficult
to raise grandchildren properly—
they are always imitating their parents.

Grandpa Dudley came for dinner and before leaving he gave his grandson $10. "Now be careful with that money, Blake," he said. "Remember the saying, 'A fool and his money are soon parted.'"

"Yes, Grandpa," replied the boy, "but I want to thank you for parting with it, just the same."

As the hero in the play slapped the heroine, a small voice in the audience was heard to ask, "Granma, why doesn't she hit him back like you do Granpa?"

"Brian! Brian!"
"What, Grandma?"
"For heavens sake, are you spitting in the fishbowl?"
"No, Grandma, but I'm comin' pretty close."

If you don't think grandkids today
know the value of money, ask one how
many CDs $50 will buy.

Grandfather: (To grandson who has stolen candy from the table): Put back that candy at once.
Jeffrey: Hush, Grandpa! Don't let all these people know how badly I have been brought up!

Arthur, age 10, walked into the men's room of a Detroit restaurant and looked at all the feet that showed beneath the cubicle doors.

After checking them all out, he approached one, knocked on it, and said in a whisper, "Mom says you can come out now. Grandaddy just paid the check."

— — — —

Kathy, age 6, was sent to visit her grandma Eustacia.

Kathy's mother told her that Grandma Eustacia was very prim and proper, and that if she had to go to the bathroom she shouldn't say, "Grandma, I've got to go to the can!" She must say, "I've got to powder my nose!"

Kathy arrived at her grandma's, and for seven whole days she was a perfect lady. Whenever she had to go to the bathroom, she said, "Excuse me, I've got to powder my nose!"

At the end of the week, Eustacia said, "I've just loved having you here. Next time you come, please bring your little sister."

"I don't think so," said the child. "She's only 3, and she still powders her nose in bed!"

Grandma Gladys shouted to her teenage grandson, watching television in the living room, "Jason, what's this condom doing on the veranda?"

"What's a veranda?" replied the boy.

If thine enemy wrongs thee,
buy each of his grandchildren a drum.

"Grandma, what happens when we die?"

"The Bible says we come from dust," she explained. "And when we die, our bodies return to dust."

Later that day, her granddaughter found a pile of dirt under the bed.

"Grandma! Come quick!" she screamed. "Somebody's under the bed, either coming or going."

Reverend Eberhardt finished a glowing message one Sunday morning. A grandmother accompanied by her young grandson, Richard, shook the minister's hand at the door and announced, "Oh, Pastor, I'm just filled with your message!"

Eberhardt turned to the little boy and asked, "Well, young man, what did you think of the sermon?"

Richard looked up at him and said, "To be honest, Pastor, I got a belly full of you, too!"

― ― ― ―

The quickest way for a grandparent
to get a grandchild's attention
is to sit down and look comfortable.

― ― ― ―

Some seniors were complaining about their grandkids. One elderly gentleman shut them all up when he said, "There's one thing you can say about children—they never go around showing snapshots of their grandparents."

"Wally," said Kilburn to his 5-year-old grandson. "You know the stork has been flying around our house lately and—"

"Gee, Grandpa," interrupted the boy. "I hope he doesn't frighten Mommy. She's pregnant, you know."

― ― ― ―

Grandpa Horton was walking down a Boston street when he saw a little boy jumping up and down, trying to reach a doorbell. Horton walked over and pressed the button for the youngster. "And now what?" he asked.

"Now," said the boy, "run like hell!"

― ― ― ―

The best way to antique your furniture
is to have several grandchildren around.

― ― ― ―

Boy to his grandfather as they watched television: "Grandpa, tell me again how when you were a kid you had to walk all the way across the room to change the channel."

A Sunday school teacher described to her class how Lot's wife looked back and turned into a pillar of salt.

"Aw, that's nothing," one little boy interrupted. "My grandmother looked back and turned into a telephone pole!"

Little Betsy was fascinated by her grandfather taking out his false teeth and brushing them, so she asked him to do it again. She stood there amazed, then demanded, "Now take off your nose!"

"Has your grandfather stopped chasing women?"

"No, but we got him to slow down. We took the tires off his wheelchair."

> Petrak: What is your grandson going to be when he graduates?
> Moore: An old man.

A college boy wrote his grandfather: "I can't understand how you can call yourself a kind grandparent when you haven't sent me a check in two months. What sort of kindness is that?"

The grandfather replied, "Sonny, that's called unremitting kindness."

Grandpa Collins was complaining to his college grandson, "There is nothing worse than being old and bent."

"Yes, there is," said the young man. "Being young and broke!"

> Never give your grandson all the
> allowance you can afford.
> Keep back some to bail him out.

Little Brandon approached his grandmother and said, "Grandma, how old are you?"

"Sweetheart, it's not polite to ask a lady her age."

"Okay," said the youngster. "Then how much do you weigh?"

"That's something you shouldn't ask, either."

"Then tell me this," asked the boy. "Why don't you and Grandpa sleep together."

With that she shooed Brandon out into the backyard. Twenty minutes later, the boy came back in the house and announced, "Grandma, you're 55 years old."

"That's right."

"And you weigh 140 pounds."

"Yes, but—"

"I even know why Grandpa won't sleep with you."

"How do you know that?"

"I saw your driver's license, and you got an F in sex."

Chapter Seven

GOBBLING GOURMETS

> *Old people shouldn't eat health foods. They need all the preservatives they can get.*
> —Robert Orben

"Honey, I found a great new restaurant," said white-haired Mrs. McDowell to her septuagenarian husband as he walked in the door from an exhausting afternoon at the Home Owners' Association meeting.

"Not tonight, dear," he pleaded. "I'm too bushed to go out."

"Can't be helped," she said cheerily. "The storm knocked out our electricity."

"But our stove isn't electric," protested the old man.

"I know that, darling," she said. "But the can opener is."

Mrs. Kowalski, 78, complained to a doctor about a stomach problem. "What did you eat for dinner last night?" asked the MD.

"Oysters," she said.

"Fresh oysters?"

"How should I know?" said Mrs. Kowalski.

"Well," said the physician, "couldn't you tell when you took off the shells?"

"Good heavens," she gasped. "Are you supposed to take off the shells?"

————

Stutzer stopped by to see an old couple he hadn't visited in a long time. "How's Wendell?" he asked the woman.

"Oh," she explained, "didn't you know he's dead? He went down to the garden to pull a cabbage for dinner. When he bent down, he fell dead, right there on the spot."

"That's terrible," replied Stutzer. "What on earth did you do?"

"Well, what could I do?" said the old woman. "I had to open a can of peas!"

Drakeford, 76, sat before the doctor and complained, "I've got this terrible problem. Everything I eat turns to gas. I just had a steak and potatoes, and it all turned to gas."

"That could be serious," declared the MD.

"But fortunately," Patterson went on, "my gas is noiseless and odorless. Can you cure it?"

"I'm sure that I'll be able to help. But first, I'm going to fit you with a hearing aid, and then I'm going to fix your nose."

————

Whitehead, 68, lately retired, came home from the golf course exhausted, but his tired eyes lighted up as he stepped inside his suburban Houston house. There stood a beautiful chocolate layer cake with seven candles on it.

"A birthday cake!" he exclaimed with pleasure. "Whose birthday is it?"

"Oh," said his silver-haired wife, "that's for the dress I got on. It's seven years old today."

————

Many young people don't
seem to realize that great truths
are spoken through false teeth.

ANNOUNCEMENT IN SUN CITY NEWSPAPER

> Will the party who invited
> us for dinner please call again—
> we lost the address.

At breakfast, Hartman's wife said to him, "We're having Bitsy's boyfriend to dinner for the first time. We're gonna have a big meal with our best dishes. So please behave. Don't eat with your knife, or you'll kill her chance for marriage." Hartman agreed.

That night at supper all went well. Hartman hardly touched a thing for fear of using the wrong utensil. Then coffee arrived. Hartman took the cup and started to pour it into the saucer. The family stared daggers at him, but Hartman kept right on pouring until the saucer was full.

Hartman raised it to his mouth, looked around the table, and said, "One word out of any of you, and I'll make bubbles!"

Jerry Clower, the consummate southern comedian, convulses crowds with this special cajoler:

Yesterday morning, the Baptist preacher was at the hospital visiting Aunt Pet. She explained to him that she had all sixteen of her teeth pulled at one time. She didn't have no teeth.

While the preacher was talking to her, he was eating peanuts that were in a bowl on the nightstand. He'd talk and he'd eat. He visited, then he got up and said, "Mrs. Ledbetter, I'll be back to see you tomorrow, and I'll bring you more peanuts."

She said, "No! No, I can't chew 'em. So don't bring me no peanuts till I get me some teeth. My gums are too tender now. What I do now is just suck the chocolate off them peanuts and put the peanuts back in the bowl right there."

Worley, 76, played with the same foursome every day. As he went to open the freezer one morning before going off to the golf course, Worley turned to his wife and asked, "What shall I take out for dinner?"

The woman smiled sweetly and said, "Me."

Wayne and Emil were sitting in the living room having their afternoon hot chocolate and cookies.

"I got a new memory medicine that's fabulous," said Wayne. "It helps with your memory. It's brand new on the market. Since I've been taking it, I remember everything."

"What's the name of it?" asked Emil.

"What's that red flower that has a long stem?"

"You mean a rose?" answered Emil.

"That's it! Rose!" he called to his wife, "what's the name of my new memory medicine?"

Mrs. Rosen joined her white-haired tablemates for breakfast at a Catskill Mountains resort hotel. The waiter approached and said, "Good morning, Mrs. Rosen, what will you have for breakfast?"

"I'd like to start with a large glass of hot water with lemon. Then I'll have some stewed prunes with sweet cream. Then give me a plate of bran flakes with an apple. And for dessert an order of figs."

As the waiter left, she turned to the other women and said, "You see, nothing for me, everything for the bowels."

Diana Flax, Carefree, Arizona's, gracious grande dame, entertains guests with this glorious giggle:

Mrs. Krebs, 77, loved chicken soup. One evening, she was spooning it up when three of her husband's friends came in. "Mrs. Krebs," said the spokesman, "we are here to tell you that your husband, Bernie, has been killed in an automobile accident."

The old woman continued eating her soup. Again they told her. Still no reaction.

"Look," said the puzzled speaker, "we are telling you that your husband is dead."

She went right on eating. "Gentlemen," she said between mouthfuls, "as soon as I'm finished with this chicken soup, you're gonna hear some scream!"

Mrs. Kalish and Mrs. Cohen, two white-haired widows, met unexpectedly in the lobby of New York's Plaza Hotel.

"Shhh," said Mrs. Kalish, "don't tell anybody, but I'm having an affair."

"Oh," said Mrs. Cohen, "and who's gonna be the caterer?"

Old Buford, a retired Little Rock lawyer, loved beans. All kinds of beans. He liked pintos, kidneys, garbanzos, limas. Unfortunately they hated him. After a meal of beans, Buford left a trail of gas that forced his wife, Cora Mae, to open every window in the house.

One morning, Cora Mae said, "It's such a real nice day, why don't you go out for a walk?" Buford left and ran into his buddy, Leland. They decided to have lunch. The special was franks and baked beans. Buford ate two orders of beans and headed home.

At the house, Cora Mae met him and said, "Now darlin', ah want yew to put on this blindfold, 'cause there's somethin' ah don't want you to see."

She tied a kerchief over his eyes and led him to the living room. Suddenly the phone rang, and she said, "Now just sit there, honey, and don't peek, ah'll be right back."

Buford began to digest the beans. They turned into gas. Buford began releasing the gas. It sounded like World War II. His wife returned and pulled off his blindfold. In the room were twenty friends who sang, "Happy Birthday to you! Happy Birthday . . ."

Baldwin, an elderly anthropologist, had just returned from a remote South Pacific island where he had been studying the eating habits of the natives. The aged scientist revealed at a gathering of colleagues that members of the tribe he had studied used palm leaf suppositories to relieve constipation.

"And how do the results compare with those from the use of civilized medical treatment?" asked one of the group.

"The results struck me as superior," replied Baldwin. "In fact, with fronds like those, who needs enemas?"

————

Grandpa Finnegan lay on his deathbed. Shawn, the youngest grandson, peeked into the bedroom for a last look at the old gent. Finnegan beckoned to the boy.

"What's that smell from the kitchen?" asked the dying man.

"Grandma's making corned beef and cabbage," replied the youngster.

"Ask her if I could have just a little taste."

The boy returned and announced, "Grandma says you can't have any. It's for the wake."

Joan Peak, the Phoenix fireball organizer, overheard this smiler at a Sun City West soiree:

Despite reaching the ripe old age of 75, Daley hated his wife's cooking. He never enjoyed any of the food she labored so diligently over for him. For over forty years, Daley complained of indigestion at every meal.

She finally convinced him to visit a doctor. After a complete physical by an internist, Daley was told he had a flucky.

He trudged home totally depressed. "What's the matter?" asked his wife.

"Doctor said I had a flucky," replied the old man.

"What's a flucky?"

"I don't know."

"Don't you think you oughta find out what it is?" charged Mrs. Daley.

Daley rushed back to the doctor and said, "Please, Doc, you gotta tell me. What's a flucky?"

"I don't know," answered the MD.

"But . . . but," stammered Daley, "after my exam, you told me I had a flucky."

"I certainly did not!" snapped the physician. "I said that you got off lucky."

Vivi Davis, the beautiful Beverly Hills novelist, beams over this bubbling bon mot:

Ginsburg, a shy, little, old man, walked into Dubin's drugstore and said to the owner, "Is it possible to fix castor oil so it can't be tasted?"

"Sure," said the druggist, "and while you're waiting, have a glass of root beer on me over at the soda fountain."

Ginsburg crossed to the counter and gratefully accepted the drink. "How did it taste?" asked the pharmacist.

"That's the best glass of root beer I ever had."

"Well, the castor oil was in it. Which proves it's possible to fix it without tasting it."

"But it was my wife outside in the car who wanted the castor oil," said Ginsburg.

After owning his drugstore for over thirty years, Dillard finally decided to renovate the place. A longtime customer approached him one morning and asked, "Has putting in that lunch counter helped your business?"

"Well," answered the old druggist, "it's tripled the sale of Alka-Seltzer."

Freda and Felix had been married forty-four years and fought only at dinnertime. "How do you like the potato salad?" she asked one evening.

"It's great," said Felix. "It tastes almost like you bought it yourself."

Harriet and Eugene, both in their late seventies, were happily retired in Los Gatos. One night Harriet said, "Would you go get me some ice cream?"

"Sure," said her husband, "what do you want?"

"Darlin', you better write this down so you won't forget."

"Don't worry, I'll remember," assured Eugene.

"I'd like some vanilla ice cream with hot fudge on it, some nuts, and whipped cream with a cherry on top."

As Eugene walked out the door, his spouse asked, "Don't you want to write it down?"

"That's all right, honey," snapped Eugene. "I'll remember."

Thirty minutes later, he came back with a large bag. Harriet opened it and pulled out a ham and cheese sandwich. She groaned. "I knew it. I told you to write it down. You forgot the mustard!"

Tobin, 76, was married for fifty-five years. One afternoon he got into a fight with his spouse and headed for the Spanish Bay Health Club to steam out. Later in the evening, he started getting hungry for his wife's good cooking and decided to phone home and maybe apologize. So he called her up.

"Hello, sweetie," he said. "What are you fixing for dinner?"

"What am I makin', you bum? Gourmet poison, that's what I'm makin'! Poison!"

"So make only one portion. I'm not comin' home."

————

The widow Kazinski kept putting it off, but after a Thanksgiving feast with her grandchildren that she hardly touched, the old woman finally had some dentures made. Three days later, she returned to Dr. Wheeler's office.

"You know those teeth you made for me?" she asked. "They're no good. They don't fit."

"Let's check your bite and see what the trouble is," said the dentist.

After performing several bite tests, Wheeler announced, "As far as I can see, they fit fine."

"I'm not talkin' about my mouth," said the old woman. "They don't fit in the glass."

Betty Jane, the waitress in a Birmingham coffee shop, served an elderly couple and noticed something very unusual. The man began to eat his meal while his wife patiently stared out the window. "Is there anything wrong with your food?" BJ asked the lady.

"No, it all looks real good," she replied.

"Aren't you afraid your food will get cold if you wait much longer to eat?" asked the waitress.

"Oh," she replied, "that's all right."

"Well, aren't you hungry?"

"Ah sure am," replied the lady, "Ah'm just sittin' here waitin' 'til mah husband gets through with the teeth."

— — — —

Abe and Morris, friends for more than forty years, finished their sumptuous dinner at the fancy East Side French restaurant.

"Listen," said Abe, "why are you always trying to impress me? So you spoke to the waiter in French! Big deal! So what good is it to know French?" Abe then turned to the waiter and asked, "What did he tell you?"

"Well, sir," said the waiter, "he told me to give you the check."

Pennington walked in the house and saw his wife of forty-eight years crying. "What's the matter?" he asked.

"The dog ate the pie I made for you," she said, dabbing away a tear.

"Don't worry," he said. "I'll buy you another dog."

————

The most popular after-dinner speech on record was made by a retired corporation president, dining with his wife alone in the privacy of their home. It consisted of one sentence containing seven words of one syllable:

"You leave them, dear, I'll do them."

————

Les and Vern were celebrating their fiftieth year of friendship at a French restaurant on New York's East Side. The two retirees began chatting about missing their longtime college acquaintance. "We should have known better," said Les. "Dave never did appreciate fine dining."

"How old is Dave?"

"He's at the age now when a girl flirts with him in the movies, she's after his popcorn."

Martha Fox, the matchless Massachusetts schoolmarm, brightens parties with this mirthmaker:

Right in the middle of the big St. Valentine's seniors' dance at a Springfield retirement residence, Rizzutti began complaining of pains in his stomach. "What did you eat?" asked the doctor.

"I had a piece of pound cake."

"But pound cake shouldn't make you sick," said the physician.

"Well," continued Rizzutti, "I went to this swell wedding this afternoon and drank plenty of Chianti and ate lots of salted peanuts and deviled eggs. Then they gave us pizza with lotsa cheese and garlic and salami. Finally dinner came, and I had three helpings of pasta with some hot sausage, fried peppers, and roasted onions on the side. After that they served the most delicious French ice cream, and I had six portions along with four dishes of chocolate mousse and two, three cups of espresso. Then I had to eat that lousy piece of pound cake, and it make me sick!"

It was lunchtime at Wolfie's Delicatessen in Miami Beach and jammed with South Florida seniors. Morrison finally found an empty table occupied only by silver-haired Silverstein. "Mind if I share the table with you?" asked Morrison.

"Not at all," said the old man.

Morrison noticed that Silverstein was not eating. His food sat untouched: a huge pastrami sandwich, an order of french fries, a large plate of cole slaw, and several sour tomatoes.

"Isn't lunch any good?" asked Morrison.

"I don't know," said Silverstein. "I can't eat. I forgot to take my teeth with me."

"Maybe I can help," said Morrison, laying three different sets of dentures on the table. Morrison tried each and finally found one that fit his mouth perfectly.

After enjoying his sumptuous lunch, he said, "Thank you very much. What good luck that I should be sitting at the same table with a dentist!"

"What dentist! I'm an undertaker!"

Chapter Eight

THE GAMEAHOLICS

> *Men may trifle with their business and their politics but they never trifle with their games.*
> —George Bernard Shaw

Kingsley ran into Sanders, his former construction foreman. "Now that you're retired," asked Kingsley, "what do you do to keep busy?"

"I go bowling or fishing or to the racetrack," replied Sanders. "Play games on my computer. We have seniors' checker tournaments at our community center."

"Sounds great."

"Yeah, and I play golf, poker, bridge—"

"Somehow I just can't picture you playing a silly game like bridge."

"Let me tell you something, the game of bridge bruises more shins than hockey."

Blake and Axel were discussing activities at the Rossmoor retirement community. "I wonder why so many married couples play bridge," said Blake.

"Well, didn't you know," said Axel, "bridge was invented by two married couples who hated each other."

————

"Charlie, is your wife playing bridge again this afternoon?"

"Of course. She and her girlfriends meet five times a week at the Activities Center."

"How can they possibly play that much?"

"Easy. Bridge is a game women play so they'll have something to think about while they talk."

————

Caleb and Ruth met through a seniors' computer dating service for widows and widowers. This was their first date. As they drove through the quiet countryside, the motor in Caleb's car began to pound and finally stopped.

"Gee," said the worried widower, "I wonder what that knock could be?"

"Maybe," said Ruth, "it's opportunity."

Babson, 72, a Denver widower, hadn't had much luck finding a woman to replace his dead wife. So he went to a computer dating bureau and picked out a beautiful young flight attendant from her photo. But they explained he couldn't meet her. He'd have to take out a gray-haired woman of 63.

"Why a woman of 63?" he asked.

"This is a union shop, and she has seniority."

Hugh, 74, and Seth, 76, were chatting over coffee. "You really like playing games on that computer?" asked Hugh.

"Yeah, I get a big kick out of it," replied Seth.

"Which is faster, a computer or a human being?"

"Wait—let me think about that."

A well-adjusted senior is one
who can play golf and bridge
as if they were games.

Herbert and Della, an elderly couple, decided to have some fun in Las Vegas and tried to check into a hotel on the Strip. "Sorry," said the desk clerk, "but all the rooms are gone except the bridal suite."

"What are we gonna do with the bridal suite?" asked Herbert. "We've been married forty-seven years."

The clerk said, "If I rented you the main ballroom, it doesn't mean you have to dance?"

Quentin, 78, loved to gamble. He gambled all his life, betting on sporting events, playing poker, and visiting the track at least once a week.

When he died, all his gambling cronies gathered in the chapel for the service. The eulogist, in an impassioned voice, intoned, "I can't believe Quent is gone. No, he's not gone. No! Quentin only sleeps. He is not dead!"

A 70-year-old buddy in the back shouted up, "I got fifty bucks says he's dead."

Ethel and Irene, two white-haired Philadelphia widows, met at the beauty parlor.

"Heard you went on one of those Gaming Casino Tours down to Atlantic City," said Ethel.

"Yeah, I love playing the slot machines," said Irene. "I hit a jackpot."

"No kidding?"

"Yes," said Irene. "But the terrible thing about hitting the jackpot on a slot machine is that it takes a long time to put the money back."

Lang, 79, and Palmer, 77, were engaged in a hot and heavy shuffleboard game aboard a Caribbean cruise ship.

"I don't mind living in a retirement community," admitted Lang, "but to tell you the truth, I like to shoot a little dice once in a while."

"When I get the urge," said Palmer, "I just drive over to Laughlin in Nevada."

"Well, we do have twelve bingo parlors in our town. All the proceeds go to fight gambling."

Baxter, a retired British businessman, flew to an Orlando assisted-living community to be present at his brother's eightieth birthday party. Now back in London, all the members of his club were clustered around him, wanting to learn something about the recreation and amusement of elderly Americans.

"Well," said Baxter, "the seniors play a lot of strange games. They played one at my brother's social center called 'Damn-it'."

"You're making that up!" exclaimed a club member.

"No, it's true," swore Baxter. "Hundreds of people have these small numbered cards. A man up on the stage calls out a lot of numbers, and finally some sweet little old lady jumps up and shouts, 'Bingo!' Then all the others say, 'Damn-it!'"

What some seniors enjoy most
about table tennis is stepping
on the ball.

Arthur had been playing tennis for over fifty years. At age 71, he never failed to win the club championship at his condominium complex in Boca Raton.

Arthur played with such vim and vigor, a neighbor commented, "You play this game like it was a matter of life and death."

"Listen," said the senior champ, "tennis is not a matter of life or death—it's more important than that."

––––

Cooke, 72, and Howitt, 74, met each morning for a walk in their Ft. Lauderdale retirement community.

One day Cooke showed up with his arm in a sling. "What in the world happened to you?" asked Howitt.

"I've got a real bad case of tennis elbow," replied Cooke. "I was playing doubles with my wife, and when I didn't return an easy lob, she got mad and hit me on the arm with her racket."

––––

SENIOR TENNIS

The only game in which
love means nothing.

At an assisted-living residence in Daytona Beach, Selwin was playing checkers in the social hall with his longtime friend, Milner.

"I gotta admit," said Selwin, "that after betting for over sixty years, I'm a lousy gambler."

"Eh, don't be too hard on yourself," said Milner. "I once lost $300 playing cards, and I was playing solitaire at the time."

Sheila, 83, and Norma, 87, residents of the Villa Fontana in San Jose, met each morning at breakfast. "Why don't you ever take a walk out in the woods?" asked Sheila.

"I'm liable to get lost," replied Norma.

"Listen, if you're ever lost in the woods, just start playing solitaire. Some old biddy is bound to show up and say, 'Pardon me, but the red five goes on the black six.'"

Boothe, 67, and Mellis, 69, were fishing from a bridge when a funeral procession drove by. As it passed, Boothe removed his hat and placed it over his heart.

Touched, Mellis remarked, "That's a real nice gesture, showing respect for the dead like that."

"Well," replied Boothe, "it's the least I could do. We would have been married forty-three years next Tuesday."

RETIREE

> A man who will sit on a pier
> fishing all day, waiting for
> a bite—then lose his temper
> if dinner is five minutes late.

Paulette, 64, and her catty neighbor, Estelle, 68, were chatting over the back fence. "Surely, you don't believe your husband's story about fishing?" said Estelle. "Notice he didn't bring any fish back."

"That's what makes me believe he was fishing," replied Paulette.

McTeer had been retired for more than ten years and spent most of his time fishing. He'd been at it all day and on the way home stopped at Fazio's Fish Market.

"Throw me five red snappers," he said to Fazio.

"Why should I throw them?" asked the owner.

"I want to be able to say to my wife that I caught them."

Ellis, 71, insisted that his white-haired wife, Agnes, come fishing with him. The next morning, they were in a rowboat out on the lake at 5:30 A.M. It was biting cold, damp, and windy. Ellis had his line over side.

Twenty minutes later, Agnes began shivering and through chattering teeth she stammered, "T-tell m-me again how much f-fun we're having. I k-keep f-forgetting."

― ― ― ―

RETIREE'S WIFE

> A thoughtful woman who has the
> steak ready when her husband
> comes home from a fishing trip.

― ― ― ―

Becker, 78, arrived back at the retirement home from his daily trip to the races. Max, one of the other residents, stopped him and asked, "How'd you do at the track today?"

"I was real lucky," replied Becker. "I found a five-dollar bill, and I didn't have to walk home."

YOU'RE NEVER TOO OLD TO LAUGH

Everybody in the Fort Pierce seniors' community knew that retirees Gibb, Clarke, Selway, and Hancock played poker every Tuesday night. Nothing short of an earthquake could stop their game. These guys loved poker.

They had just begun their weekly session when Hancock toppled over and died.

Selway stood and silently intoned a prayer. Clarke got hysterical and screamed, "What'll we do?"

Gibb remained calm. "Take out the deuces and treys," he said.

RETIREMENT CLUB CARD ROOM

Where men are men and spades
are double.

Loretta belonged to a Miami Mah-Jongg club. She played with wives of other retirees, and the women gambled quite heavily at the games.

One night Loretta arrived home past midnight and didn't want to wake her husband. She undressed completely in the living room and, handbag over her arm, tiptoed into the bedroom—only to find her husband sitting up in bed, reading.

He took one look at her and exclaimed, "Good Lord! Did you lose everything?"

Milsome, 72, and his wife, Stella, 68, were driving home from the weekly card game. "I hate playing bridge with a bad loser," said Milsome.

"I agree," said his wife. "But I'd rather play with a bad loser than with any kind of a winner, any day."

Morrie was celebrating his eightieth birthday. His buddy, Burgess, asked him, "How does it feel to be 80?"

"I feel great—played thirty-two holes today—on my harmonica."

GOLF

A game in which a little white ball
is chased by men too old to chase
anything else.

The best golfer at a retirement village was 80-year-old Lenville. He could hit the ball over 200 yards every time. However, he was losing his eyesight and couldn't follow the trajectory of his ball.

One day he was introduced to another 80-year-old who was not as good a golfer but had 20/20 vision. "I got a great idea," said Lenville. "Let's play together. You can see well enough to tell where my ball lands."

On their first day out, the long hitter stepped up to the ball and hit it 275 yards. Carpenter shouted, "I see it! I see it!"

"Where'd it go?" asked Lenville.

"I forgot!" admitted Carpenter.

————

Sunday is the day when seniors
bow their heads. Some of them are
praying, and some of them are putting.

————

Dodge, 81, and Grissom, 82, were taking their morning stroll around the peaceful upscale Sequoias retirement settlement in Portola Valley.

"My grandson got a job as a caddy at a country club," announced Dodge. "Is there much money at that?"

"Well," replied Grissom, "the salary ain't much, but they make a lot extra backin' up fellas when they lie about the scores they made."

"Good Lord! I think your partner is having a stroke!"

"Just so he doesn't get it on our scorecard!"

Gerry Ford was the first person to make golf a contact sport. When he yelled, "Fore!" you never knew if he was telling people to get out of the way or predicting how many spectators he was going to hit.

—Bob Hope

To some men in retirement, the whole point of the day is to get the figure on the golf score down as low as the one on the Social Security check.

OVERHEARD IN A RETIREMENT VILLAGE CLUBHOUSE

"Believe me, it's not that I cheat," explained the golfer. "It's just that I play golf for my health, and a low score makes me feel better!"

Wallace and Duffy were annoyed by an unusually elderly twosome in front of them. One of the pair diddled and dawdled on the fairway, while the other was searching diligently through the rough.

"Hey," shouted Wallace impatiently, "why don't you help your friend find his ball?"

"He's got his ball," replied the old man. "He's looking for his club."

————

Many a retiree who doesn't
play golf can't give it up.

————

Margarete, 67, recently joined the senior womens' golf club at Oakmont's retirement community in Santa Rosa. This was her first chance to break a score of 125, but she had to sink a 10-foot putt to accomplish the feat.

Quivering with excitement, she crawled around the green for five minutes, studying each blade of grass in the path of the ball, then fluttered a handkerchief to determine the exact direction of the wind. Finally Margarete appealed to her long-suffering cart companion, "Lenore, how should I putt this?"

"Keep it low!" was the reply.

SENIOR DUFFER

One who addresses the ball twice—
before and after swinging.

————

As Guthrie returned home from a day at the links, his young grandson asked, "Well, Gramps, did you win?"

"Let me put it this way," he replied. "Your grandfather got to hit the ball more times than anyone else."

————

Did you hear about the retired golfer in Pebble Beach who was so used to cheating that when he got a hole-in-one he put down a zero on his score card?

————

Josephine Bonnett, Wyoming's plucky pioneer woman of the nineties, overheard this conversation in the clubhouse of the Saratoga Inn:

Norma, 68, and Claudette, 67, were heading back to their cars after a long afternoon on the course.

"I swear I don't know why we let Adelaide join our womens' senior golf group. She's a terrible golfer."

"Come on now," said Claudette. "Is Adelaide really that bad?"

"Bad? She's the only woman in the world who has an unplayable lie when she tees up!"

> Senior golfers say
> they shoot their age. It's
> probably more like their weight.

Cindy Chennault, Idaho's famous film beauty, fractures friends with this cute fable:

Kenton married the prettiest widow in the retirement village, and having recently discovered golf, was introducing his bride to the game. He spent hours telling her about what great exercise golf was, the beauty of the countryside, and the joy of being out in the open.

On the first tee, Kenton prepared to give his wife a demonstration of the game itself. Taking his driver in hand, he swung hard and missed. Embarrassed, he adjusted his stance, swung again and whiffed. On his third try, he missed again.

At this point, Mrs. Kenton asked, "Honey, I can see that golf is great exercise. And it sure is pretty out here. But what's the little white ball for?"

> You can always tell the senior golfers
> in church. When they put their hands
> together to pray, they use the
> interlocking grip.

Brent, 66, and Terry, 69, signed on for a seniors' golf tour package to Europe and were playing a mountainous course in the Swiss Alps. After playing a particularly difficult lie at the bottom of a crevasse, Brent rejoined his partner.

"How many?" asked Terry.

"Three."

"Three? I heard six!"

"They were echoes."

A senior duffer is one
who constantly passes the cup.

Jessica, 66, and Laverne, 64, were two of the bitterest golf rivals in a San Jose retirement community. Neither woman trusted the other's arithmetic. One day they were playing a heated match and watching each other like hawks.

After holing out on the fourth green and marking her six on the scorecard, Jessica asked her opponent, "What'd you have?"

Laverne went through the motions of mentally counting up. "Six!" she said and then hastily corrected herself. "No—a five."

Calmly Jessica marked the scorecard, saying out loud, "Eight!"

"Eight? I couldn't have had eight."

"Nope. You claimed six, then changed it to five. But actually you had seven."

"Then why mark down an eight?"

"One stroke penalty," said Jessica, "for improving your lie."

> Many seniors use carts instead
> of caddies because carts can't
> count, criticize, or laugh.

The new clubhouse at the Rancho Cañada course in Carmel was jammed with nineteenth-hole retired revelers. Suddenly cranky, craggy old Brandon entered the room and complained to a group of seniors. "That Cameron cheats," he cried. "He lost his ball in the rough and played another ball without losing a stroke."

"How do you know he didn't find his ball?" asked a friend.

"Because I've got it in my pocket."

LONGEVITY

Age is a quality of mind.
If you have left your dreams behind,
If hope is lost;
If you no longer look ahead,
If your ambitious fires are dead
Then you are old.
But if from life you take the best,
And if in life you keep the jest,
If love you hold,
No matter how the years go by,
No matter how the birthdays fly
You are not too old.

YOU ARE NOT OLD.

ABOUT THE AUTHOR

This is Larry Wilde's fiftieth joke book, and with sales of over 12 million copies, it is the largest-selling series of its kind in publishing history. The New York Times calls him "America's best-selling humorist."

Larry is also the author of The Great Comedians Talk About Comedy and *How the Great Comedy Writers Create Laughter,* recognized as the definitive works on comedy technique.

A former stand-up comedian, Larry Wilde is now a motivational speaker. He provides programs for corporations, associations, and healthcare professionals, showing how humor can alleviate stress, build team spirit, open communication, and add immeasurable pleasure to work and to life.

He is the founder of National Humor Month and the director of the Carmel Institute of Humor, which sponsors research and roundtables to explore laughter as a vital tool for wellness, productivity, and the quality of life.

Larry lives on the California coast with his wife, author Maryruth Wilde.

THE MYSTERIES OF MARY ROBERTS RINEHART

THE AFTER HOUSE	(0-8217-4246-6, $3.99/$4.99)
THE CIRCULAR STAIRCASE	(0-8217-3528-4, $3.95/$4.95)
THE DOOR	(0-8217-3526-8, $3.95/$4.95)
THE FRIGHTENED WIFE	(0-8217-3494-6, $3.95/$4.95)
A LIGHT IN THE WINDOW	(0-8217-4021-0, $3.99/$4.99)
THE STATE VS. ELINOR NORTON	(0-8217-2412-6, $3.50/$4.50)
THE SWIMMING POOL	(0-8217-3679-5, $3.95/$4.95)
THE WALL	(0-8217-4017-2, $3.99/$4.99)

THE WINDOW AT THE WHITE CAT
(0-8217-4246-9, $3.99/$4.99)

THREE COMPLETE NOVELS: THE BAT, THE HAUNTED LADY, THE YELLOW ROOM
(0-8217-114-4, $13.00/$16.00)

Available wherever paperbacks are sold, or order direct from the Publisher. Send cover price plus 50¢ per copy for mailing and handling to Penguin USA, P.O. Box 999, c/o Dept. 17109, Bergenfield, NJ 07621. Residents of New York and Tennessee must include sales tax. DO NOT SEND CASH.

WILLIAM H. LOVEJOY
YOUR TICKET TO A WORLD OF POLITICAL INTRIGUE AND NONSTOP THRILLS. . . .

CHINA DOME	(0-7860-0111-9, $5.99/$6.99)
DELTA BLUE	(0-8217-3540-3, $4.50/$5.50)
RED RAIN	(0-7860-0230-1, $5.99/$6.99)
ULTRA DEEP	(0-8217-3694-9, $4.50/$5.50)
WHITE NIGHT	(0-8217-4587-5, $4.50/$5.50)

Available wherever paperbacks are sold, or order direct from the Publisher. Send cover price plus 50¢ per copy for mailing and handling to Penguin USA, P.O. Box 999, c/o Dept. 17109, Bergenfield, NJ 07621. Residents of New York and Tennessee must include sales tax. DO NOT SEND CASH.

WILLIAM W. JOHNSTONE
THE ASHES SERIES

OUT OF THE ASHES (#1)	(0-7860-0289-1, $4.99/$5.99)
BLOOD IN THE ASHES (#4)	(0-8217-3009-6, $3.95/$4.95)
ALONE IN THE ASHES (#5)	(0-8217-4019-9, $3.99/$4.99)
WIND IN THE ASHES (#6)	(0-8217-3257-9, $3.95/$4.95)
VALOR IN THE ASHES (#9)	(0-8217-2484-3, $3.95/$4.95)
TRAPPED IN THE ASHES (#10)	(0-8217-2626-9, $3.95/$4.95)
DEATH IN THE ASHES (#11)	(0-8217-2922-5, $3.95/$4.95)
SURVIVAL IN THE ASHES (#12)	(0-8217-3098-3, $3.95/$4.95)
FURY IN THE ASHES (#13)	(0-8217-3316-8, $3.95/$4.95)
COURAGE IN THE ASHES (#14)	(0-8217-3574-8, $3.99/$4.99)
VENGEANCE IN THE ASHES (#16)	(0-8217-4066-0, $3.99/$4.99)
TREASON IN THE ASHES (#19)	(0-8217-4521-2, $4.50/$5.50)
D-DAY IN THE ASHES	(0-8217-4650-2, $4.50/$5.50)
BETRAYAL IN THE ASHES	(0-8217-5265-0, $4.99/$5.99)

Available wherever paperbacks are sold, or order direct from the Publisher. Send cover price plus 50¢ per copy for mailing and handling to Penguin USA, P.O. Box 999, c/o Dept. 17109, Bergenfield, NJ 07621. Residents of New York and Tennessee must include sales tax. DO NOT SEND CASH.